QUEEN OF QUARK

The Ultimate Quark Guide
and Cookbook

HHBI
PRESS

Copyright © 2019 by HHBI LLC.

ISBN 978-1-7328949-0-7
HHBI Press, a division of HHBI LLC.
Printed with passion in Europe

Acknowledgements

This book is the result of a transatlantic story of passion, friendship and the endless delights of healthy eating and living. It would have not been possible to realize the dream of a first time ever global Quark Guide without the support and encouragement of our families, friends and Quark Lovers from around the world, and of course everybody at HHBI press.

Therefore we would like to express our sincere and heartfelt thanks to all of you. Thank you for having joined us in our mission! A big thank you also to our mothers, who have done so much for us throughout their entire lives and taught us how to cook healthily. Can you believe that we turned our passion into writing a cookbook?

We dedicate this book to all mothers, and to all who want to be the best version of themselves, who want to cherish their body, nourish their good intentions, and make smart decisions concerning health and happiness.

Content

PART 4: THERAPEUTIC TREATMENTS

PART 5: WEIGHT LOSS WITH QUARK

What others say

Finally! As a German living in the United States I have missed Quark a great deal. Now I know where to find it and get so many delicious recipes on top. Thank you Queen of Quark!

K. Braun, Florida, USA

It was 2010 when I first travelled to Finland to complete my Master's degree in nutrition science and see first-hand why obesity and rates of type 2 diabetes were relatively low in Scandinavian countries. What I didn't expect was the Finns heavy consumption of a food that was not quite cheese and not quite yogurt... yet just as satisfying as both. This dairy food is called rahka, or quark as we call it in English. These days I work as a Dietitian in Sweden, Finland's neighbor. Quark (or kvarg in Swedish) is widely popular, particularly in the health and fitness communities. You can always find it in gyms and convenience stores, and advertised on billboards as 'nature's protein supplement'.

Based on its unrivalled nutritional profile and tasty creamy texture, I'm surprised that quark is still under the radar of nutrition experts and health food enthusiasts in North America and the UK. I'm really pleased that quark will now - with this beautiful book from Queen of Quark© - be introduced to the rest of the world. It definitely deserves a regular spot in your fridge.

Joe Leech, Dietitian
MSc Nutrition & Dietetics, Founder
www.dietvsdisease.org

The Ultimate Quark Guide & Cookbook unlocks the many secrets of using Quark - a traditional German dairy superfood. Contained in these pages are delicious recipes that feature Quark, such as smoothies, dressings, dips and desserts, alongside methods of using Quark for face masks, bath soaks, and sunburns. With this unique book from the Queen of Quark©, you will enjoy exploring the many possibilities of quark in your kitchen and beyond.

Maggie Green,
RDN, LD Culinary Dietitian and
Cookbook Author, The Green Apron
Company

Quick Start Guide

No matter whether you are a long-time Quark fan or an absolute Quark newbie, this book was written for you. Its intention is to assist you in integrating the healthy superfood Quark into your life to add more wellness, happiness and pleasure, spoon by spoon. This guide will introduce you to the many possibilities of incorporating Quark into your daily life, starting with healthy breakfast recipes, on to delicious cheesecakes and dessert recipes and even to using Quark in beauty applications and natural remedies, all which anyone can do at home, on a limited budget and without any prerequisite knowledge.

Whatever interests you about Quark – from all-natural facials to your personal weight-loss plan, you can find the answers here.

AT A QUICK GLANCE, HERE ARE THE MOST IMPORTANT TOPICS:

I was a kid when I first discovered Quark. I was stung by a wasp and my grandmother, Her Royal Highness, Sophia, Queen of Quark, put a thick layer of cold Quark, fresh from her refrigerator, onto the swelling. It immediately cooled the sting and soothed the pain. I stopped crying and was amazed! "What's that Grandma?" I asked. She gently smiled at me and said: "This is the main ingredient of your favorite breakfast pancake. It is called Quark." That was the day when my joyful culinary journey with Quark began.

Delicious, low-carb, high-protein eating and healing are just two of the main qualities of my all-time favorite food. My two human alter egos are nutritionists and I know they eat Quark daily. And they also recommend it to their clients. As a kid, the awkward sounding name Quark always reminded me of a little frog trying to pronounce a new word. Over the years, Quark has given me endless culinary joys, wonderful low-carb tastes, amazing beauty boosts and powerful health benefits.

Ever since my childhood in beautiful Bavaria I always searched for more clean eating ingredients and secrets. During my adult life, as I was traveling the World, I was overjoyed to now find Quark in over 30 countries. So today, after all those years as a Quark Lover, and having stepped up to the throne of my Mother Anna, it is an honor and a joyful duty for me to share the Goodness of Quark with you in this first time ever Quark Guide and Cookbook. I hope you enjoy my recipe collection and use the hidden secrets of Quark for your personal health and happiness.

Get ready to Quark up your life! I feel honored to guide you. After you finish reading this book I will accompany you on your journey towards personal health, happiness and beauty. You are royally invited to join me at www.queenofquark.com and connect 24/7, read my blog and get free coupons. Enjoy your Ultimate Quark Guide and Cookbook!

Yours sincerely,

Queen of Quark

(and her human alter egos) Kerstin 'KP' and Linda

Food choices are health choices

QUEEN OF QUARK

Introduction

In the last few years, the popularity of Quark has skyrocketed outside of its country of origin, Germany, and for a good reason. The all-natural, high-protein, low-fat alternative to soft cheese or yoghurt increases your protein intake in many delicious ways, while supporting happiness, weight loss and well-being. Is Quark a new medical miracle? The answer is yes and no. Quark is not new. It has been known and used in many European countries for over 500 years. The first mentions of Quark are over 5000 years old. And yes, Quark has powerful healing qualities that keep surprising our modern technology driven society. Lindsay Vonn, the US Olympic skier for example revealed in an interview 2010, that she had experienced Quark in Austria, where it is called Topfen. After she suffered a severe muscle bruise during her training, the Austrians wrapped her shin in "Topfen". This reduced pain and swelling. This positive effect impressed Vonn and left her enthusiastic about Quark, and many scientists in the US surprised.

In Europe though the therapeutic effects of Quark have been know since hundreds of years and until today Quark is even used in many hospitals and rehabilitation facilities in order to reduce the pain for arthritis and rheumatic patients. Many doctors know that the caseine in Quark has great qualties like cooling and supporting anti-inflammatory processes. But Quark is much more then that. It is also a so called "mood food" since protein and tryptophan have mood enhancing properties.

Can food make you happy? Yes. And what, for that matter, is healthy food? Every day new, allegedly super-healthy foodstuffs appear on the market. Uncountable commercials promise us perfect well-being, beauty and happiness, if we buy the right product. The same goes for diets of all kinds. Even worse, many strange-sounding food labels reputed by scientific studies and a multitude of contradicting press releases add to the confusion. It is hard to reach a well-informed decision concerning the ideal food regimen. What is the right food? How do you find orientation in this flood of contradicting information?

An answer is provided by renowned scientists and institutions, including the American Diabetes Association, the Institute of Integrative Nutrition in New York and the British Heart Foundation. International food research and science based independent nutrition information portals like Diet vs. Disease help you find

Let Food
be thy medicine
and medicine
be thy Food

HIPPOCRATES

orientation in the contradictory information. They have proven, for instance, that the human body is able to create the so-called "happiness hormones", serotonin and tryptophan from amino acids which are contained in Quark. Many researchers confirm these findings and also underline the importance of protein for the human body. The smart choices we make concerning what we eat and drink every day, have an enormous influence on our well-being, how much energy we have, whether we lose weight or not, and even how we feel.

According to Yale-trained physician Aviva Romm, at least 80% of Americans do not get the nutrients they need for basic health standards. In spite of all kinds of negative news referring to the steady rise of diet-related illnesses such as cancer, Alzheimer's and diabetes, one basic insight repeats itself: the ideal diet foregoes bad fats, artificial additives and sugar. In fact the ideal diet comprises everything the human body needs for a healthy metabolism, a life without food-related diseases, and a stable weight level: vitamins, minerals, protein, and fibers. The trick to a healthy, well-balanced diet lies within the combination of the right food, its content and variety. Our author's answer to one of the most pressing questions of our time is: Trust nature and eat clean! The more unprocessed the food, the better.

Quark is an all-natural product, loaded with protein, probiotics, minerals, and the definitely happiness-inducing tryptophan. Utilize the power of protein! In comparison to yoghurt or Skyr, the health effects of which are undisputed, Quark gives better results and contains almost three times as much protein. Many of these positive properties are listed in this guide, together with tasty recipes, smart substitutions, cures and therapeutic applications.

So what can Quark do for you? In this book you will find everything you need to know about Quark and the many ways it can be used to promote health, weight loss and beauty. The 5 Parts of this book have been designed for you to easily explore and find the chapters that appeal to you the most. Part 1 covers the history, production and the health benefits of Quark. Part 2 introduces you to the broad variety of Quark recipes for baking, cooking and blending. Part 3 will surprise you with many tried and tested beauty treatments using Quark, which are practically unknown outside of Europe. Part 4 visits the wonderful uses of Quark in therapeutic treatments and remedies. Part 5 opens the door to utilizing Quark's huge dietary potential: the use of its high protein content for a no-hunger, long term sustainable weight-loss success.

This book will deliver protein-packed recipes and directives right to your home and show you that the popularity of Quark is much more than a fleeting food trend

in these health-conscious times. Its versatility, smoothness and delicious tanginess will make it your indispensable companion to a healthy, happy lifestyle. So in the future, whenever you want to add some protein to your favorite dish or smoothie, think of the little frog of The Queen of Quark© and let this book be your guide to Europe's secret Superfood that you can enjoy now in your home, or wherever you may be.

PART 1

Understanding Quark

Think yoghurt but less sour and with more protein. Think cheese but with less fat.

Now you're heading towards something that Europeans have cherished for centuries: Quark. This high protein, low fat alternative to soft cheese and yoghurt is mild in taste, creamy in texture and extremely versatile in use. It is a perfect low carb ingredient for sandwiches, cheesecakes, dressings, spreads, smoothies, salads, soups and, as you will discover, even healing. There is no limit to the creative uses of Quark in baking, cooking, blending or topping. It can be eaten sweet or savory, hot or cold. Quark has also been used for generations as a base in many home remedies and is loved for its support in weight-loss efforts. Be surprised, and delve into the long heritage of this European Superfood now.

QUARK – A VERSATILE NATURAL WONDER

Modern lifestyles and industrial food production have changed the traditional way of cooking tremendously. Much of the food we consume is too high in sugar, fat, artificial flavors and many other unhealthy ingredients while important ingredients like minerals are lacking. Quark is protein-packed, low in sodium, low in fat, and high in valuable minerals and vitamins. An all-natural, mild soft cheese, Quark offers a great opportunity for everyone seeking a healthier way of eating without sacrificing on flavor.

Due to its low fat and low sodium content, Quark is often used as a health conscious and taste boosting substitute for sour cream and cream cheese that merges perfectly with sweet, sour and savory tastes. If you live in the US, Canada or the UK you might have not heard about or seen it yet, but watch out! In health-conscious times, it is no wonder that Quark, the European Superfood is now hitting supermarket shelves around the world, even in the US. It is simply a perfect ingredient to use anywhere from dressings to dips, cheesecakes to ice cream, smoothies to breads and so much more. Even Pizza tastes better with Quark. And, as a fat free add-on to great taste, you cut back on carbs and heart unhealthy fats.

The history of Quark goes as far back as the 14th century. Nutritionists believe it to have been discovered accidentally in Germany when milk turned sour due to lack of cooling. Today we know that probiotic products like Yoghurt, organically sourced and professionally produced, are very beneficial for the human body. And, in recent times, the popularity of these products has skyrocketed. Same thing goes for Quark. The difference being that Quark contains much more valuable protein than yoghurt, takes much longer in the production process to develop the superb taste and has a less sour taste to it.

WHAT EXACTLY IS QUARK?

Quark is an all natural low fat, high protein multipurpose dairy product with a mild, tangy flavor to it. Although it can be produced from cows' milk, sheep milk or goats' milk you will find it most commonly produced from cows' milk. Quark is a non-GMO probiotic product with a high protein and mineral content, which makes it very valuable for the human body. It is 100% gluten free, kosher and vegetarian friendly and should not (always depending on the dairy) contain any added sugar,

Great
days start
with great
Food

QUEEN OF QUARK

fillers, gelatin or artificial ingredients. Producing Quark is relatively simple; you can even do it at home. All you need is milk, an enzyme and probiotic live cultures that can be bought online. And of course you need quality milk in order to receive quality Quark. So, please be aware of the quality of the milk when you buy Quark or produce it at home. The basic ingredient equation for the milk used in Quark is simple: the happier and healthier the animals, the better the milk. High-grade feed results in first-class nutrients that will serve your body optimally.

Quark is often produced by adding rennet and bacteria cultures to the milk although some dairies either do not use rennet, substituting buttermilk or lemon juice instead, or use vegetable rennet in order to keep the product vegetarian friendly. Whey is a liquid by-product of the production of Quark and also has many positive health and beauty promoting qualities. You will find recipes for that in Part 3.

TIP FROM THE QUEEN
Use Quark to replace unhealthy foods like sour cream and cream cheese. You reduce the amount of fat you eat and boost your protein intake! Remember, Protein is the cornerstone for healthy long-lasting weight loss.

USEFUL FACTS AND A LITTLE HISTORY

The history of milk consumption by humans goes back over ten thousand years. In many cultures milk was a symbol for fertility and immortality. The people of India for instance, believed that the world originated in a sea of milk.

Quark has been known to mankind for at least 5,000 years. Mainly in the countries of northern Europe, it quickly became a favorite food and remedy. Like many other good things in life, it was discovered by accident as the bacteria in the milk started to do their work. Soon it was produced on purpose, mainly in Bavaria, Norway or Austria. Archeological discoveries prove that people have been producing and loving Quark for a long, long time!

Quark is known in Europe under many different names and for many different uses. In some areas in Southern Germany Quark is called *Bibbeleskäs,* in East

Prussia it is called *Glumse*. In Austria Quark is called *Topfen*, in Norway it is called *Kvark*. Whereever and however you enjoy Quark, its high-protein and low-fat content will blow you away and open new doors to healthy eating! Dare to experiment and enjoy the journey!

A EUROPEAN SUPERFOOD GOES GLOBAL

There's a lot of talk about Superfoods, but it's often unclear what they are and on which grounds this term is used. Also it seems that often the term is used in a marketing-smart way in order to simply sell more of a specific product. Many experts – including myself – stick to a more profound definition of Superfoods which is backed up by scientific research. We would call foods such as avocados, blueberries, quinoa and also Quark Superfoods because they offer consumers an unsurpassed abundance of health benefits based on their nutrient-density per calorie.

Superfoods contain high amounts of vitamins, minerals, antioxidants and valuable bacteria which are often missing in a typical diet. That's why it makes good sense to include a wide array of different Superfoods into your daily diet.

Looking at Quark with its mild taste, creamy texture and high protein content, it is no wonder that its popularity has recently been growing exponentially. In the 1980's there was no Quark anywhere to be found in the US. Europeans all across America were missing their Quark and not just as an ingredient for the famous German Cheesecake. See recipe on page 122. Now times have changed. More and more dairies now produce Quark and supermarkets in America and Great Britain sell Quark, in plain as well as flavored varieties including coconut, mixed berries and vanilla. More and more consumers are falling in love with Quark. One of the reasons for this Guide is to promote knowledge about the broad variety of health promoting recipes and applications with Quark.

Take a look at this A-Z Superfood list, that also serves as a great add-on or base for your Quark dish, smoothie or pie.

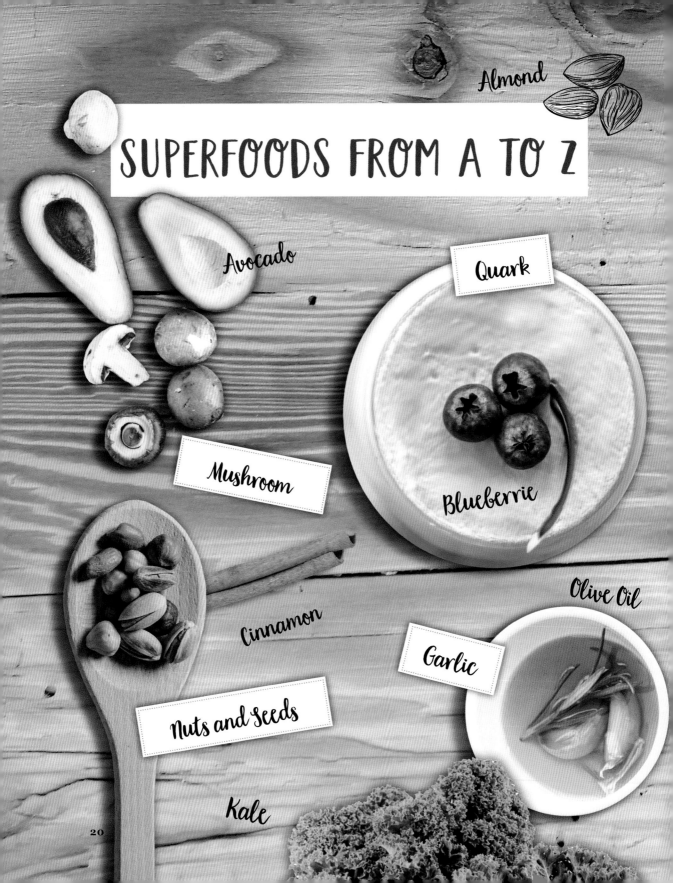

SUPERFOODS FROM A TO Z

Almond

Avocado

Quark

Mushroom

Blueberrie

Cinnamon

Olive Oil

Garlic

Nuts and Seeds

Kale

20

Coconut

Chillie

Tomatoe

Chia Seed

Dark Chocolate

Pomegranate

Beans

- ★ Almond
- ★ Avocado
- ★ Beans
- ★ Blueberrie
- ★ Chia Seed
- ★ Chillie
- ★ Cacao
- ★ Cinnamon
- ★ Coconut
- ★ Dark Chocolate
- ★ Fermented Food
- ★ Fruit
- ★ Garlic
- ★ Ginger
- ★ Jalapeno
- ★ Kale
- ★ Mushroom
- ★ Nuts and Seeds
- ★ Olive Oil
- ★ Pomegranate
- ★ Papaya
- ★ Quinoa
- ★ Quark
- ★ Red Wine
- ★ Tea
- ★ Tomatoe
- ★ Whole Grain
- ★ Zucchini

ANOTHER SUPERFOOD: SAY HELLO TO WHEY –
THE VALUABLE BY-PRODUCT WHEN MAKING QUARK

Whey contains lactose and is the liquid that is left over when Quark is produced. It is super healthy. Whey is low-calorie and has several commercial uses including in sports drinks and beauty products. In Part 2 of this Quark Guide you will find recipes for the use of this healthy Superfood and other valuable tips in and the Beauty Application Section in Part 3.

HEALTH BENEFITS AND SMART SUBSTITUTIONS

A lot of Quark Lovers around the world call Quark their "smart food". The reason for it is simple. Due to its low fat, low salt and high protein content, Quark is an ideal substitution for unhealthy foods like cream cheese and sour cream, without affecting taste. Typically German Cheesecake is made with Quark rather than with cream cheese, which drastically reduces the calories and the unhealthy fat content. Plus Cheesecake made with Quark is light and fluffy.

Top 10 health-smart substitutions with Quark:
- Replace Sour Cream with Quark on baked potatoes or Tacos with Quark
- Forget Cream Cheese and use Quark for your favorite spread
- Replace your Greek Yoghurt with Quark in your smoothies and increase your protein intake
- Use Quark instead of butter or mayo on your sandwich. Quark is very spreadable and tastes great savory or sweet
- Use Quark instead of sour cream in your salad dressings
- Drop a spoonful of Quark into your soup and cut out on the unhealthy fats of sour cream by doing so
- Use Quark instead of butter or margarine for baking muffins or pancakes.
- Add Quark instead of sour cream to your pizza
- Replace flour with Quark when you bake bread. It adds fluffiness and taste!
- Freshen up your guacamole with Quark instead of sour cream. Your waistline and cholesterol level will thank you for it!

Quark is simple in its ingredients but high in valuable nutrients for the human body. Besides the high protein and low sodium content, many valuable minerals, vitamins, amino acids and important trace elements like zinc, iron or folate are contained in Quark. The list of nutrition facts shows:

QUARK IS A TRUE SUPERFOOD

Quark contains:
- Proteins
- Essential amino acids
- Milk fat
- Lactic acid
- Lactose
- Minerals, particularly calcium
- Trace elements
- Vitamins A, D, and E (lipo-soluble)
- Vitamins B and C (soluble in water)

The composition of these contents in Quark and whey is the secret to their great power, their good taste, and their significant health effects. No wonder these foods also work in favor of beauty and happiness! Looking at the amino acid components in Quark it becomes obvious why Quark is called a *"mood food"*. The essential amino acid Tryptohan is known as a mood messenger and also serves several other important purposes, like nitrogen balance in adults and growth in infants. It also helps the body produce niacin, which is essential in creating the neurotransmitter serotonin. Serotonin helps us experience elevated levels of happiness, reduces the feeling of stress and promotes good, deep sleep which, as we all know, is so important for our well-being and nightly rejuvenation. So a smoothie or dish prepared with Quark will not just nurture your body it will also improve your mood. And as the American author Madeleine L'Engle said: "Laughing heals a lot of hurts!"

THE MOST IMPORTANT NUTRIENTS IN QUARK

	low-fat Quark (less than 10% fat / 100 g)	Whey (100 ml)
Protein	14 g	0.8 g
Fat	0 g	0.2 g
Carbohydrates	4 g	4.7 g
Sodium	40 mg	45 mg
Potassium	140 mg	130 mg
Calcium	120 mg	60 mg
Magnesium	11 mg	8 mg
Phosphorus	190 mg	43 mg
Iron	400 µg	90 µg
Fluoride	17 µg	10 µg
Zinc	600 µg	130 µg
Vitamin A	3 µg	6 µg
Vitamin B1	40 µg	40 µg
Vitamin B2	300 µg	140 µg
Vitamin B6	60 µg	40 µg
Vitamin C	700 µg	1,000 µg
Vitamin E	20 µg	2 µg
Folic acid	30 µg	1 µg
Tryptophan	176 mg	16 mg

WHAT MAKES THESE NUTRIENTS SO VALUABLE?

Vitamin A has a positive impact on the immune system. It supports the body when sores need to heal, it strengthens the bladder and the eyes, and is also helpful for bone growth. Vitamin A is a lipo-soluble vitamin.

Vitamin B soothes the nerves. It promotes the build-up of muscles, helps digestion, and aids in tissue repair. It strengthens the liver, stimulates the metabolism, and will therefore also help the body with fat reduction. In addition, it has a positive effect on the brain and a person's mood. The group of B-vitamins belong to the water-soluble vitamins.

Vitamin C is important for the immune system, the connective tissue, the gums, and it supports the power to concentrate. It plays a part for the build-up and preservation of skin, bones, and teeth, making it an important factor for tissue repair, too. Vitamin C is water-soluble.

Vitamin E is needed for the blood and its coagulation. It has a strengthening effect on the eyes and, just like Vitamin C, works as an anti-aging formula.

Minerals

We wouldn't be able to exist without minerals and trace elements like iron or zinc. It is important that we give our body enough of them – and Quark is a healthy and delicious supplier of minerals. Good health can taste so good!

Sodium is needed to regulate the body's water balance and its blood formation; it balances pH levels as well.

Potassium is needed for the body's energy supply. It also plays an important part in regulating the body's water balance, helps metabolize protein, and supports a healthy cardiovascular system.

Calcium is vitally needed for the build-up of teeth and bones; it is important for the regulation of the cardiovascular system, blood coagulation, and the transmission of impulses between muscles and nerves.

Magnesium supports nerve transmission, helps muscle function and allows the body to utilize its energy supply efficiently. It is also important for bones and teeth.

Phosphorus is important when it comes to blood coagulation and the body's energy metabolism, and helps to balance pH.

Trace elements belong to the category of minerals. In our body they only appear in minuscule amounts, the so-called "trace". Iron, fluoride, iodine, and zinc are essential for life and they must be received via our food because the body is not able to produce them. By eating Quark, you supply your body with these necessary nutrients without a lot of calories.

Proteins

They are the basic elements of every kind of body cell. Without proteins, the body cannot survive. Essential amino acids must be consumed within our food as the body is unable to produce them.

Tryptophan is one of those essential amino acids which works like a natural mood enhancer because it helps the body to create certain hormones like serotonin, melatonin etc. Foods which are rich in tryptophan will calm you down, support a relaxing sleep, and reduce anxiety and depression.

LIVING SMART AND HEALTHY WITH QUARK

Did you know that hair and skin are mostly protein? Also your muscles, the hemo-globin in your blood and your brain cells are made out of protein. Protein is life and without protein life as we know it would not be possible. The question is: What kind of protein and which amount of protein should be included in an optimal diet? The answers to these questions vary widely but bottom line according to most sources is that the US Department for Agriculture (USDA) and also most health organizations recommend to go lean with protein (which means to choose low fat versions) and to vary the protein choices (meaning using both animal and plant based protein). The latest research also shows that the quality of the protein makes a big difference.

Health is
the greatest gift,
contentment
is the greatest
Wealth

BUDDHA

As you have seen, Quark contains some true health warriors. That's why Quark is so highly cherished in many countries like Germany, Austria, Norway, Sweden and Poland. It is also why it is going global with its Superfood powers.

One other benefit of eating Quark regularly is that it strengthens your intestinal flora and promotes "oh so important" gut health. Scientists know that a healthy intestinal flora will not only aid in a problem-free digestion, but also promote a strong immune defense for an active metabolism and well-being in general. Even beautiful skin depends on a healthy gut flora. And, one of the key success factors to weight loss is a good metabolism.

With Quark (and whey), it's not just about eating. You can also apply both products externally, so they can work their healing magic and visually enhance your appearance.

Some of Quark's Positive Benefits when used externally:
- Stimulating the blood circulation
- Skin-cleansing
- Regenerating the skin
- Skin-strengthening
- Skin-refreshing
- Cooling
- Helping the skin to maintain a good pH level
- Soothing pain of sprains, stings and swelling
- Anti-inflammatory

In short: Quark promotes a healthy lifestyle from the inside as well as the outside.

WHERE DO I FIND QUARK?

In more than 36 countries, Quark can be found as a standard product in the dairy section. But in countries like Canada or the U.S., Quark is not yet available in every supermarket, although the number keeps growing. From Wholefoods in the US to Sainsbury's, Tesco in the UK and Woolworth's in Australia, more and more supermarkets now carry Quark in their dairy sections. Most likely you will find it in the refrigerated section, near yoghurt, ricotta or mozzarella cheese. If you do not find it in your home town, please check in with the store manager as many stores are willing to order Quark if their customers request it. Also, if nothing works, go Quark shopping online or make your own Quark at home. You will find the recipe on page 150. What is the difference between Quark and other dairy products?

THE TOP 5 DAIRY PRODUCTS AT A GLANCE

Buttermilk
Like whey, buttermilk is a by-product in dairy product manufacture. While whey is left over when Quark is made, buttermilk is the result of making butter. It has less than 1 per cent fat and is high in lecithin, calcium and phosphor.

Ricotta cheese
Ricotta looks a little bit like Quark, but it's different. It is made from the proteins within the whey, so it is a by-product of Quark production. The name basically means cooked once more.

Skyr
Skyr has been made in Iceland for hundreds of years. It is similar to yoghurt in it's protein content which means it contains considerably less protein then Quark.

Sour Milk
Sour milk is more fluid than yoghurt. Yet another kind of bacteria culture is responsible for it, the so-called mesophilic germs. Unlike yoghurt bacteria, they do not need higher temperatures to become active. They start their process at 28 – 30° Celsius (about 82° – 86° Fahrenheit). In former times, sour milk just happened by itself as the acidic cultures within the milk began to turn it sour. Nowadays, milk is treated before it may be sold and bacteria are killed– the bad ones as well as the useful ones.

Yoghurt
You might mistake Quark for yoghurt or Skyr, but there are clear differences in its nutrient value as well as the production process and in the taste. Yoghurt tastes more tart than Quark and has also a slightly different texture. Also, the bacteria used to make yoghurt are different from the ones you would need for Quark.

HERBS AND SPICES THAT COMPLIMENT THE TASTE OF QUARK

Oregano

Curry

Cumin

Spring Onion

Peppermint

Parlsey

Chive

Dill

Thyme

30

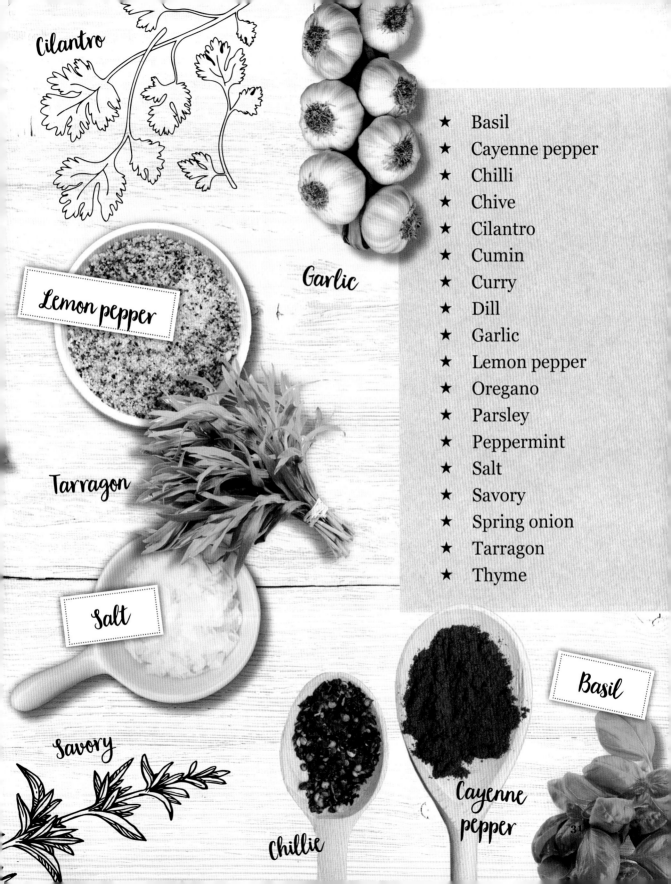

Cilantro

Garlic

Lemon pepper

Tarragon

Salt

Savory

Chillie

Cayenne pepper

Basil

- ★ Basil
- ★ Cayenne pepper
- ★ Chilli
- ★ Chive
- ★ Cilantro
- ★ Cumin
- ★ Curry
- ★ Dill
- ★ Garlic
- ★ Lemon pepper
- ★ Oregano
- ★ Parsley
- ★ Peppermint
- ★ Salt
- ★ Savory
- ★ Spring onion
- ★ Tarragon
- ★ Thyme

31

FREQUENTLY ASKED QUESTIONS - FAQ

Why is Quark so good? Whoever enjoys dairy products like yoghurt (and has no problem digesting them) will appreciate the many positive properties of Quark. The advantages of Quark include:

- High in protein
- Low in calories
- Great taste
- Many valuable nutrients
- Low fat
- Low carb
- No artificial additives – Quark is a natural product
- Mood food (Quark enhances your mood)
- Satisfies your hunger for a long time

Is Quark gluten-free? Yes, absolutely.

Is Quark well suited for vegetarians? Yes it is. Depending on the producer, Quark is vegetarian friendly and most dairies only use vegetable rennet. To be sure, please check the label on the product.

Does Quark have probiotic qualities? Yes, most Quark brands are naturally filled with live and active probiotics that are beneficial to your digestive system.

What about Quark and allergies? Quark is safe for people with corn, nut and soy allergies. Only people with a lactose intolerance must be careful.

What is lactose intolerance? Some people lack the lactase enzyme which is necessary to digest lactose, the kind of sugar that milk contains. You may have some of the lactose enzyme but not in sufficient amounts to digest dairy products. If so, this group of people should turn to lactose-free Quark, if available. There is no reason for lactose-intolerant persons to not use Quark as an externally applied remedy or cosmetic product.

Consequences of lactose intolerance: Because the enzyme is missing, the lactose cannot be processed in the stomach. It reaches the colon in an undigested condition and causes problems. Flatulence and belly-aches are the most common symptoms, but can also include cramps and sudden bouts of diarrhea. For others, there might be more diffuse symptoms such as generally feeling unwell, chronic fatigue, states of depression, headaches, or aching limbs. How wonderful that you can forego these symptoms by choosing lactose-free products!

How is Quark different than yoghurt? Quark is produced like a cheese and different cultures are used. Quark has more protein then most yoghurts and also has a less sour taste.

I have heard dairy products should be avoided? There has been a lot of confusing and differing information on a variety of food groups and even nutrition experts seem unable to agree on the arguments on dairy. The author of this Quark guide believes in the concept of Bio-Individuality that has been created by Joshua Rosenthal, Director of the Institute of Integrated Nutrition and taught by many holistic health experts. Bio-Individuality is based on the belief that there is no one perfect way of eating that works for everyone. Each person has very specific needs for his or her own health according to age, constitution, gender, weight, size, lifestyle and ancestry. So this guide suggests that you eat a variety of foods including high-quality dairy, fruit, fish, meat and vegetables that serve your body, and avoid the rest, including industrial sugar, sweeteners and trans fats. To find out what works best for you, listen to your body and in case of uncertainty consult with your doctor.

ASK THE QUEEN

Whenever you have a question about Quark; please feel free to reach out to the Queen via facebook, twitter or by email. Her mission is to help you "Quark up your life".

Cooking, Baking and Blending

Quark is healthy, slimming, and rich in proteins which makes it also a very attractive food item for vegetarians. Whether you use it for smoothies or baking, hot or cold, as a main ingredient for dips and sauces, as a smart replacement for sour cream in soups or as a topping for baked potatoes, is healthy and delicious. Its low fat and high protein content makes it a perfect guilt free food for use any time of the day.

In Part 2 you will find a selection of tried and tested recipes for various occasions, which are easy to prepare, from breakfast in the morning to a late-night snack. You can find many more on my blog at queenofquark.blog.

> **TIP FROM THE QUEEN**
> *Please use common sense while cooking and handling hot pots, pans and ovens. Do not let children handle pans or cook unsupervised! Give them the opportunity to help in preparing and actively partaking in preparing the meals.*

No one is born a great cook, one learns by doing

JULIA CHILDS

Easy Breakfasts

"A good day starts with a good breakfast", nutritionists know. A good breakfast doesn't have to take long to prepare – it should just be nutritional and tasty! Remember: This first meal of the day sets your energy level, mood and concentration for hours to come.

Quark Breakfast Bowl

What better way to start the day than with a bowl of Quark combined with fresh fruits, berries and nuts? You can even add oatmeal. Or cereals. It's a crunchy breakfast treat which gives you plenty of energy for a busy morning. How about breakfast favorites for the whole family? Try this one:

Serves 2

INGREDIENTS:
1 cup strawberry Quark
½ cup Blueberries
1 teaspoon oats
1 teaspoon coconut flakes
1 tablespoon strawberry jam

Mix all ingredients in a blender and pour into bowl. Decorate with blueberries, oats and coconut flakes.

Fluffy Quark Pancakes

Serves 4

INGREDIENTS:

2 eggs
1/2 cup flour
1/2 cup Quark
1 tablespoon sugar or stevia
Vegetable oil or Quark butter for frying

Mix ingredients in a bowl and stir. Heat the oil in a pan, ladle dollops of batter into it, fry at medium temperature until golden brown. Together with Quark and fresh fruit, this is a real power breakfast.

TIP FROM THE QUEEN

In order to get the sweetness into a Quark dish without the calories, use products like stevia or Erythrit. It benefits your health in a much better way than regular sugar. Also, honey is a great alternative to maple syrup for kids over age 3 and adults, too!

Fruity Quark Pancakes

If you enjoyed the fluffy pancakes, try these as an alternative - They are just as delicious – but fruity! All you need is:

Serves 4

~~~~~~

INGREDIENTS:
1 tablespoon Quark
1 egg
Fresh fruit (e.g. strawberries)

~~~~~~

Just mix the quark with the egg in a bowl and sweeten to taste. Pour equal portions of the mixture into your heated frying pan and turn over when golden brown. Serve with fresh fruit and enjoy!

Best ever Banana Pancakes

Did you or your family love the pancakes in the previous recipes? Then try this Banana Pancake recipe and let me know what you think!

Serves 4

INGREDIENTS:
1 banana peeled and mashed
2 eggs
1 tablespoon sugar
1 tablespoon vanilla extract
1/2 cup Quark
zest of a lemon
pinch of salt
1/2 teaspoon cinnamon

Mix the banana with the eggs, Quark, lemon zest and vanilla sugar. Add the cinnamon, salt and some low-fat milk, if needed for a more fluid consistency. Heat a pan, put some butter in it and add a tablespoon of the mixture to the pan to form pancakes. Flip over when golden brown and fry the other side. Serve warm with fresh fruit or maple syrup.

TIP FROM THE QUEEN
Use medium heat so as not to let the butter turn brown which will change the flavor.

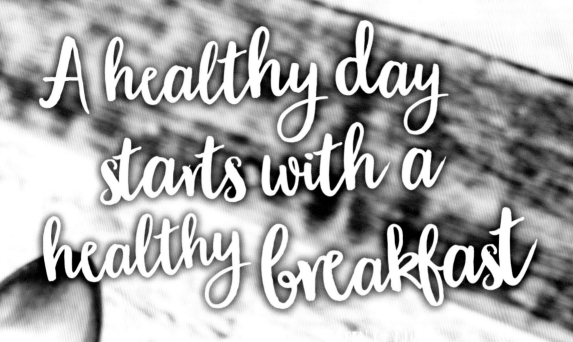

A healthy day starts with a healthy breakfast

Protein-Packed Smoothies
Green Power Smoothie

Serves 1

INGREDIENTS:

100 g strawberries
1 cup fresh spinach
1 cup fresh kale
½ cup Quark
Apple juice if desired for additional sweetness

Put strawberries, spinach and Quark into a blender and mix thoroughly. Add apple juice until it reaches a thick, fluid consistency. Pour into a glass and enjoy!

Banana Chocolate Smoothie

This delicious high protein Smoothie will make you feel fuller for
longer and gives you a perfect start into an energized day.

Serves 2

INGREDIENTS:

1/2 cup fresh Quark
1 banana, peeled and sliced
1 tablespoon vanilla powder
1 tablespoon chocolate protein powder
2 teaspoons flax seeds
3 tablespoons cup cocoa powder
2 cups ice

Put all ingredients in blender and blend until smooth. In case you need more liquid,
add low-fat milk or almond milk.

Blueberry Avocado Smoothie

This Smoothie is the perfect boost for firm skin, healthy muscles and a beautiful body!

Serves 1

INGREDIENTS:

1 cup low fat milk
1 1/2 cups frozen blueberries
1/2 avocado pitted and peeled
1 banana
1 cup Quark
Vanilla extract

Combine the milk, blueberries, banana and the avocado in the blender and blend till smooth. Add the Quark and vanilla extract and blend again for approx. 5-10 seconds. Serve immediately and enjoy!

JB — The Junior Boost

Loved by kids around the world - loaded with valuable calcium.

Serves 2

INGREDIENTS:
1/2 cup Quark
1 peeled banana
1 tablespoon honey
1/2 cup crushed ice
1 cup milk or almond milk
1 teaspoon oats

Place all ingredients in a blender and mix well.

Carrot Ginger Smoothie

Carrots hold powerful benefits for your eyes, skin and
immune system, and when combined with Ginger and Quark,
is a true Superfood Smoothie.

Serves 1

INGREDIENTS:
1 cup fresh Quark
1/2 fresh carrot juice
1/2 cup grated carrots
1/2 cup fresh orange juice
1 tablespoon fresh lemon juice
1 drip of olive oil to help your body utilize the vitamin A out of the carrots
1/4 teaspoon grated ginger
(if you don´t like ginger, simply replace it with chopped parsley)
1 tablespoon pumpkin or flaxseeds (optional)
salt

Combine the Quark with the carrots, oil and juices in a blender. Blend until smooth
and then add the seeds and ginger. Salt to taste. Enjoy!

Coconut Almond Smoothie

This Coconut Almond Smoothie is perfect for your sweet afternoon protein boost. It not only rewards your sweet taste buds but also boosts your health since almond nuts are a rich source of vitamins, minerals and packed with numerous health promoting phytochemicals.

Serves 1

INGREDIENTS:
1 tablespoon shredded coconut
1 tablespoon sliced almonds
3/4 cup Quark
1/2 cup almond milk

Place all ingredients in a blender and mix till smooth. Enjoy!

Green Detox Protein Smoothie

This low-carb, easy-to-make smoothie will help cleanse and detox your body.

Serves 2

INGREDIENTS:
1 cup strong green tea (chilled)
2 leaves fresh spinach
1/4 cup Quark
1 teaspoon honey or sweetener
1/2 cup ice cubes

Simply blend all ingredients together and add more ice if needed for a thicker texture.

Mango Quark with Chia Seeds and Oatmeal

Here's a recipe for a healthy start to the day with this fresh Mango Quark, sprinkled with energy-boosting chia seeds and whole grain oatmeal. It's a perfect source of protein, vitamins A, C and E, as well as minerals, including potassium, magnesium, copper, calcium and phosphorus.

Serves 1

INGREDIENTS:
2 cups Quark
1 mango, peeled and chopped
1/2 cup milk
Sugar or sweetener
1 teaspoon chia seed
1 tablespoon oatmeal

Peel the mango and cut it into smaller pieces. Combine the Quark, milk and mango in a blender and mix it well. Sweeten to your personal taste. Sprinkle with chia seed and oatmeal. Add chopped nuts if you like, for an extra boost of magnesium and enjoy!

The Superfood Breakfast Bowl

Combine the powerful superfoods chia seeds, blueberries, papaya,
coconut, Quark and Cinnamon to create a healthy morning pleasure
that will boost your energy all day long.

Serves 2

INGREDIENTS:
1/2 cup frozen papaya
1/2 cup frozen pineapple
1/2 banana sliced
1/2 cup fresh or frozen blueberries
1 teaspoon chia seeds
1/2 cup coconut water
1/2 cup coconut milk
1/2 cup Quark
Pinch of cinnamon
Add honey for sweetness if desired

FOR THE TOPPING
1/2 banana sliced
2 tablespoons shredded coconut

Blend the frozen and fresh fruit with the coconut milk, the cinnamon, Quark and coconut water in the blender until smooth. Pour the smoothie into a bowl and garnish it with the topping. Serve immediately and enjoy!

Good Food is the entrance door to good health

QUEEN OF QUARK

Soups, Salads and Dressings

Quark is a perfect and extremely tasty, low-fat ingredient for soups and dressings. Just use it to replace sour cream or whipped cream for a broad variety of hot or cold dishes. You will discover: Healthy eating can taste great!

Carrot Coconut Soup

Sometimes there is nothing better than a hot cup of soup, right?
This vegetarian and gluten-free choice might become your best
companion on those chilly days.

Serves 4

INGREDIENTS:

1 tablespoon coconut oil
1 medium onion, peeled and chopped
1 tablespoon grated ginger, fresh
1 teaspoon minced garlic
1 teaspoon ground turmeric
1 small fresh chilli pepper, seeded and chopped
6 peeled and chopped carrots, organic if possible
1/2 cup potatoes, peeled and sliced thickly
5 cups vegetable broth
1/2 cup canned coconut milk
3 tablespoons fresh Quark
Sea salt
Freshly grounded black pepper

In a large pot, heat the coconut oil and add the garlic, chilli and ginger. Stir until translucent and then add the carrots and potatoes. Add some salt and fresh pepper and stir for about 3 minutes. Then add the broth, coconut milk and turmeric. Bring the soup to boil and reduce the heat to let the soup simmer for about 20 minutes. Use a food processor or blender to puree the soup. Return the soup to the pot on low heat, season with salt and pepper and garnish with your extra dose of protein; good, low-fat Quark. Serve immediately. If you wish, serve with whole wheat bread or whole wheat crackers. Enjoy!

Chilled Onion Soup

This chilled onion soup is centered around an ingredient that Victoria Jarzabkowski, a nutritionist with the Fitness Institute of Texas at the University of Texas in Austin, calls "super healthy" and any nutritionist would agree. It also tastes delightful.

Serves 4

~~~

INGREDIENTS:

1/4 cup Quark
3/4 cup of buttermilk
1 garlic clove and 3 shallots or 1 sweet onion, finely chopped
Salt and black pepper
2 tablespoons of fresh chives, finely cut
1 teaspoon butter

~~~

Cook the onion with the garlic and some of the chives in a pan until golden brown. Set aside and let it cool down. Mix the Quark with the buttermilk, adding the rest of the chives, salt and pepper. Combine all ingredients and refrigerate. Serve chilled, with a healthy salad or whole grain bread as a side. Enjoy the refreshing taste and the vast amount of health-promoting phytochemicals.

Potato Mushroom Soup

This creamy potato mushroom soup is a perfect treat for any cold day
and it is made avoiding the typical fat and cholesterol that is often
found in creamy soups.

Serves 4

INGREDIENTS:

1 pound potatoes, cooked
1 onion, chopped
1 carrot, peeled and chopped
1 celery stalk
5 large mushrooms, washed, peeled and sliced
2 tablespoons virgin olive oil
2 teaspoons fresh parsley or fresh cilantro, chopped
3 cups vegetable broth
2 cups water
3/4 cup Quark
1/2 cup low fat milk
Salt and pepper

Mix the Quark with the milk in a small bowl and add a pinch of salt. Cook the potatoes and vegetables in water and add the broth later. In a separate skillet heat the oil and add the sliced mushrooms. Fry till golden brown and set aside. When the potatoes are soft (after approximately 20 minutes) strain and puree with a handheld blender. Pour in the Quark and milk mixture and stir. Add fresh pepper and salt as needed, and the herbs. Top with the mushrooms, serve hot and enjoy!

Protein Power Pea Soup

Here's a healthy soup recipe, packed with valuable fiber and protein.

Serves 4

INGREDIENTS:

1/4 cup Quark
1 tablespoon olive oil (extra virgin if possible)
1 onion, chopped
1 stalk celery, chopped
1 cloves garlic, chopped
1 teaspoon fresh thyme or parsley, chopped
3 cups peas, fresh or frozen
1/2 cup water
2 cups chicken or vegetable broth
Pepper, salt

Heat the olive oil, add the onion and celery, and stir occasionally until softened. Add garlic and herbs, and after one minute stir in the peas. Add the water and broth and bring it to a boil. Reduce heat to low and simmer until very tender, about 1 minute. Puree the soup in a blender, add the Quark, and blend again until smooth. At the end add salt and pepper to taste. Enjoy!

Pumpkin/Butternut Squash Soup

If you think of turning the pumpkins of Halloween into a delicious
soup or simply love butternut squash then this is your recipe.
It's high in dietary fiber and vitamin C.

Serves 4

INGREDIENTS:

1 large onion minced
2 large butternut squash peeled, seeded and chopped
2 apples cored and chopped
2 tablespoons fresh ginger minced
2 cloves minced garlic
3 cups vegetable broth
2 cups water
1 teaspoon salt
1/2 teaspoon black pepper
1/2 cup Quark
2 tablespoons olive oil (cold pressed)

Heat the oil in a large pot and cook the onions, garlic and ginger for 3 minutes.
Add the broth, the water, the apples, salt and pepper and let it boil until the squash
softens (approx. 20-30 minutes). Pour the mixture into a blender and blend until
smooth. Add more water, salt and pepper if needed. Pour the mixture back into
your pot and let simmer for 3-5 minutes. Serve your soup hot, garnish it with Quark
and fresh herbs, like chopped parsley or cilantro. Enjoy!

Italian Tomato Soup with Quark

Same as the classical tomato soup but with Quark instead of sour cream. Smart!

Serves 2

INGREDIENTS

12 ounce ripe tomatoes
1 onion
1 tablespoon fresh Quark
1 carrot
1 celery stick
1 garlic clove, crushed
2 tablespoons olive oil (virgin if possible)
2 teaspoon tomato purée
2 bay leaves
Salt and fresh pepper
Vegetable stock

Firstly, prepare your vegetables. Wash and cut the tomatoes into quarters, peel the onion and carrot and chop them into small pieces. Chop the celery stick, and heat olive oil in a large pot. Combine the onion, carrot, garlic and celery and mix them together. Cook the vegetables, on low heat, until they're soft and faintly coloured.

Add the tomato purée and tomatoes, then stir it and sprinkle in a good pinch of salt and pepper. Tear 2 bay leaves into a few pieces and throw them into the pot. Stir to mix everything together, put the lid on the pot and let the tomatoes stew over a low heat for 10 minutes until they shrink down in the pot and their juices flow nicely. From time to time, give the pot a good shake – this will keep everything well mixed. Then pour in the vegetable stock, stir, and turn up the heat until everything is bubbling.

Let it boil for 3 minutes then turn the heat down to low and continue to cook gently for 15 minutes, stirring occasionally. Remove the pot from the heat and ladle the soup into your blender until it's about three-quarters full, fit the lid on tightly and turn the machine on full. Blend until the soup is smooth and pour the puréed soup back into the pot.

Reheat it over a medium heat and stir in the Quark, salt and pepper. Reheat gently and serve hot, with another dollop of Quark in the middle.

Homemade Coleslaw

Often coleslaw in supermarkets is loaded with fat, calories, artificial flavors and unhealthy preservatives. Here is a recipe for a super healthy, homemade, creamy coleslaw.

Serves 4

INGREDIENTS:

1 pound shredded white cabbage
1/2 cup shredded carrots
1/2 cup shredded apple (can be left out if you want to keep it simple)
2 cups fresh Quark
1/4 cup organic apple cider vinegar
Juice of half a lemon
2 teaspoons Stevia or any other sweetener
1 tablespoon mustard
2 tablespoons onion powder
Pinch of salt and pepper

In a large bowl, mix the apple with the carrots and the cabbage. Combine the other ingredients in a different, small sized bowl and pour the mixture over the cabbage. Mix well and chill for an hour. Enjoy this healthy version of coleslaw. And please, share the recipe if you like it!

Cucumber Salad with Quark

This recipe is SO easy to make, and delicious too. Enjoy!

Serves 4

INGREDIENTS:

1 cucumber
1 small onion
Chives and fresh dill depending on your taste
1 cup Quark
2 ounce whey
1 tablespoon freshly pressed lemon juice
Salt, pepper
1 tablespoon chopped walnuts

Wash the cucumber and dice it. Peel the onion and dice it finely. Chop the herbs finely. Put all ingredients into a bowl and mix thoroughly. Let it sit for 10 minutes and enjoy!

TIP FROM THE QUEEN

Lemon juice is a natural flavor enhancer. It often adds the certain "extra" to your dish and is sugar-free, unlike most vinegars.

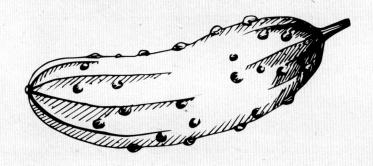

Kale and Apple Salad

This salad is ideal for a light lunch and it can be prepared at home...
low carb to go, packed with valuable vitamins!

Serves 2

INGREDIENTS:
2 tablespoons extra virgin olive oil
2 teaspoons apple cider vinegar
2 teaspoons Quark
Juice of 1/2 lemon, freshly squeezed
5 cups torn kale leaves (big ribs removed)
1 apple, cut into small pieces
Salt and pepper

Combine the olive oil, vinegar, Quark, lemon juice, salt and pepper in a jar or small bowl and stir. Pour the sauce over the kale leaves in a large salad bowl and mix thoroughly. Add the apples, some walnuts and blue cheese crumbles on top of the kale if you wish. Lightly toss to combine. Enjoy!

Avocado Asparagus Strawberry Salad

Here's the recipe for a savory salad that will boost your energy and nurture your body with healthy, beauty-promoting fats.

Serves 2

~~~~~~

INGREDIENTS:

1-2 ripe avocados, peeled, pitted and chopped
1 package green asparagus
10-15 large strawberries, washed and sliced
1 teaspoon white balsamic vinegar
1 tablespoon Quark
1 tablespoon extra virgin olive oil (cold pressed)
1 package of mixed salad (e.g. spinach or salad blend)
Salt and pepper
2-4 fresh basil leaves
Walnuts, if desired

~~~~~~

Heat the olive oil in a pan. Cut off the hard ends of the asparagus and discard. Cut the remaining asparagus in smaller pieces. Fry for 2-3 minutes. In a separate bowl, mix the washed and cut strawberries with the peeled and chopped avocado. Add salt and pepper and mix the ingredients with the balsamic vinegar and Quark. Pour over the heated asparagus. Add the chopped basil leaves and walnuts. Pour over the washed salad and get ready for this delicious and super-healthy meal. Add additional dressing sparingly if desired. Enjoy!

Easy-To-Make Salad Dressing

Shelf bought salad dressings are often filled with artificial flavors, fats and sugar. The solution? Mix your own dressing in just 2 minutes! It´s easy, saves money and is much healthier than what you would typically find on super market shelves. Simply mix 3 tablespoons extra virgin olive oil with 3 tablespoons Quark in a small bowl, add 1/2 teaspoon minced fresh ginger and 2 teaspoons of balsamic vinegar. Add salt and pepper and, if you like the fresh taste of lime, the zest of 1/2 lime. You can also add any herbs you like since they add extra nutritional value, e.g. chives, parsley, cilantro. Refrigerate until needed, stir before use and simply pour over your salad.

Mediterranean Salad Dressing

This Mediterranean Salad Dressing is a true delight that
you can prepare in just 5 minutes.

Serves 2

INGREDIENTS:
1 lemon, juiced
1 tablespoon white wine vinegar
1 clove garlic, can be left out
1/2 cup fresh Quark
1/3 cup olive oil, extra virgin if possible
1/2 teaspoon mild mustard
1/2 teaspoon salt
1/4 teaspoon black pepper, freshly ground
1/2 teaspoon fresh dill, finely chopped
1/2 teaspoon jives, washed and chopped

Combine all ingredients in a bowl, save
some herbs as a remainder for decoration,
and whisk well to combine. Refrigerate until
ready to serve and decorate with the remaining
fresh herbs.

Delicious Dips and Spreads

Adding protein to your favorite dip or spread is easy: Just add Quark and use the 0% version if you want to make sure you go low-fat.

Herb Quark

Serves 2

INGREDIENTS:

1 cup Quark
1 tablespoon freshly pressed lemon juice
4 tablespoons herbs of the season
1 clove of garlic
Salt, pepper

Peel the garlic and mince finely. Mix Quark with all ingredients, season to taste with salt and pepper and let it sit for a while. Add Herb Quark as a fresh dip to vegetables, meat, or with potatoes boiled in their skin, as a complete meal.

The New Avocado Chili Dip

This is the perfect, innovative appetizer and dip for any party,
and it is not overloaded with unhealthy fats. Great with vegetable
sticks or crackers!

Serves 4

INGREDIENTS:

2 avocados
1/2 lemon or 1 lime, juiced
2 tablespoons chopped onion
1 tablespoon Quark or yoghurt
1/2 teaspoon salt
1 clove garlic
1/2 fresh chili, chopped and seeded
10 leaves fresh cilantro chopped

Cut the avocados into halves. Remove the center and scoop out the pulp into a small bowl. Use a fork to mash the avocado. Stir in lemon juice, onion, Quark, salt and herbs. Cover the bowl, and refrigerate for 1 hour before serving. Enjoy!

Black Bean Protein Dip

Black beans are known to improve fat metabolism and are high
in fiber, which is good for anyone trying to lose some weight
or looking for a healthy, anytime snack.

Serves 4

~~~~~~~~~~~~~~~~~~~~~~~~~~~~~~

INGREDIENTS:

1 can black beans, drained (15 ounces)
1/2 cup Quark
1/4 cup tomato paste
1/2 cup finely chopped tomatoes
1/2 teaspoon cumin
1/4 teaspoon cayenne pepper (add more if you wish it to be real spicy)
Pinch of salt
Fresh cilantro chopped

~~~~~~~~~~~~~~~~~~~~~~~~~~~~~~

Mash the beans in a bowl until it is chunky and then add the Quark, tomato paste,
cumin, cayenne pepper and fresh tomatoes. Mix well and refrigerate for minimum
1 hour. Enjoy your dip with veggie sticks, pita bread or rice crackers.

Horseradish Quark Topping

This topping is easy to prepare, delicious in taste, and low in fat.

Serves 2

INGREDIENTS:
1/2 cup of Quark
Mashed potatoes (produced from 2 large boiled potatoes)
1 tablespoon low fat milk
Salt and black pepper
2 tablespoons of horseradish (fresh or powdered)
If you are not a fan of horseradish, you can substitute 2 cloves of crushed garlic and chopped chives.

Mix all ingredients in a bowl and place the topping on boiled or roasted vegetables or potatoes. Then place everything in an oven at 390 degrees Fahrenheit and heat until topping is crisp.

Tomato Basil Dip

We promise, you will not feel guilty reaching for
a second serving of this fantastic dip.

Serves 4

INGREDIENTS:

2 tomatoes, seeded and chopped
1 tablespoon fresh basil, chopped
1/2 teaspoon onion powder
1/2 teaspoon white pepper
1 clove garlic, minced (optional)
1/2 teaspoon onion powder
3/4 cup Quark
1 spring onion, finely chopped
Pinch of salt

Combine the Quark with the herbs, tomatoes and spices in a large mixing bowl.
Beat with an electric mixer for about 1-2 minutes. Feel free to also add some
Worcestershire sauce if desired, and mix again. Refrigerate for at least an hour
before serving and sprinkle it with spring onions, finely chopped.

The Onion Party Dip

Here's a party favorite that goes great with tacos, chips or veggie sticks!

Serves 4

INGREDIENTS:
1 large yellow onion (chopped)
1/4 teaspoon cayenne pepper
1 teaspoon extra virgin olive oil
1 cup fresh Quark
3 green onions (chopped)
Salt and pepper
Sparkling water for smoothness

Heat the olive oil and add the yellow onions. Cook for approx. 15 minutes or until tender and golden. Add the cayenne pepper, stir and let it cool. In a separate bowl mix the Quark with the salt, pepper, green onions. Add the cooked onions and mix well. Serve with crackers, chips or - the healthier choice- with veggies. Enjoy!

Oktoberfest Quark

Experience the taste of the famous Munich Oktoberfest at home!
Treat yourself with the Queen's family recipe of Oktoberfest Quark.
It is low-carb, low-fat, high in protein and of course super tasty!
By the way: it is also a great spread on bagels, or a perfect
topping for baked potatoes.

Serves 4

INGREDIENTS:
2 cups of Quark
1 bunch chives
Salt
2 teaspoons sparkling water

Wash, pat dry and cut the chives into small pieces. Add the Quark and salt, mix in bowl by hand or with a mixer. Add the water if you desire a more creamy texture.

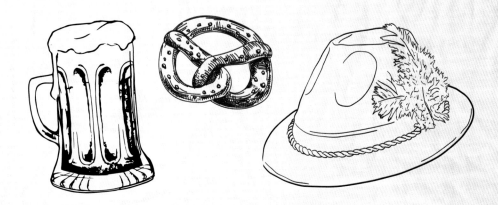

Pumpkin Seed Quark Spread

This is a perfect, protein packed appetizer or side that goes well with vegetables, tacos or even a steak.

Serves 6-8

INGREDIENTS:

1 ounce pumpkin seeds
1 garlic clove
1/2 bunch parsley
7 ounces Quark
1 tablespoon pumpkin seed oil
Salt
Pepper

Toast the pumpkin seeds in a small skillet, stirring frequently, until fragrant and beginning to pop. Remove from heat and let cool. Set aside about 1/4 of the pumpkin seeds for garnish. Chop the remaining seeds. Peel the garlic and finely chop. Rinse the parsley, shake dry and cut into slices diagonally. Mix the chopped pumpkin puree (seeds, pumpkin puree, garlic) and parsley in a bowl together with the Quark and pumpkin seed oil. Season with salt and pepper. Garnish with reserved pumpkin seeds. Serve with whole-wheat bread - or baked potatoes, as desired.

French Port Wine Quark Butter

Quark butter exists in hundreds of delicious variations,
all much lower in fat then pure butter.

Makes 14 portions butter

INGREDIENTS:
1 stick butter, slightly softened
3 tablespoons fresh Quark
2 tablespoons port wine
Pinch of freshly ground pepper to taste
1 teaspoon herbs de Provence, optional

Mix all of the ingredients in a large bowl with a fork until you reach a homogenous creamy consistency. Store in an airtight container. Can be refrigerated up to 3 weeks.

Vegetarian Delights

Quark is a vegetarian friendly ingredient and with its high protein content is an ideal food for anyone who is looking to add protein to their meals.

Quark Dumplings

Quark dumplings are very tasty in a hearty beef broth. You can also use them to add a special touch to a carpaccio.

Serves 4

INGREDIENTS:
1 cup low-fat Quark
3 tablespoons breadcrumbs
4 tablespoons flour
2 eggs
2 tablespoons finely minced parsley
Pinch of salt
2 liters of salted water

Put Quark into a clean cloth to let the liquid drain off. Mix all ingredients and let the batter sit for 30 minutes. Bring the salted water to a boil. Use two spoons to form dumplings and let them glide into the boiling water, boil up briefly and then let them simmer for 8 minutes at medium heat.

The Veggie Pan

Here's a perfect lunch which can be prepared in only 25 minutes!

Serves 4

INGREDIENTS:

2 lb. pounds mixed vegetables, e.g. broccoli, zucchini, cauliflower, bell peppers
chopped into pieces
4 small tomatoes
1 lb. small potatoes, cut in half or quarters depending on the size
8 ounce Quark
3 tablespoons butter or 1/4 cup coconut oil
1 chopped onion or scallions
Salt or Sea Salt
1 tablespoon rosemary (best when it´s fresh)
Extra virgin olive oil
2 tablespoons fresh chives
2 tablespoons fresh parsley

Place the veggies & potatoes in a pan and sprinkle rosemary and olive oil over them. Place the pan in the oven and bake at 390 degrees Fahrenheit for 20-30 minutes. Remove from oven and let cool.

The Quark Dip: Mix the Quark with the herbs and salt. Add pepper and garlic as your tastebuds desire.

Red Beet Carpaccio with Horseradish Quark

This is a beautiful appetizer, loaded with valuable minerals, folate and vitamins.

Serves 4

INGREDIENTS:
2 red beets
1 cup Quark
2 tablespoons horseradish
Salt and pepper

Wash red beets thoroughly, wrap in aluminum foil and bake in the oven at 390 degrees Fahrenheit for 40-50 minutes depending on their size. Let them cool and slice finely. Place the slices on a plate as you would with the classic meat carpaccio. Mix Quark and horseradish and season to taste with salt and pepper. Add little dollops to the beets and enjoy!

Quark Gnocchi with a Zucchini Tomato Sauce

Get the sunny tastes of Italy with these small,
palate-pleasing dumplings!

Serves 4

INGREDIENTS:
For the Gnocchi
3/4 cup of Quark
2 cups flour
3 eggs, beaten
1 tablespoons dry yeast
1/2 cup seminola
1/2 cup milk, warmed
1 tablespoon butter, at room temperature

Mix the flour with the warm milk and yeast. Put it aside and cover it for about about 30 minutes. Then mix it with the Quark, eggs and seminola. Create finger size sausages, cut them in smaller pieces and bake on high temperature until golden brown. If you would like to add sauce to your gnocchi, my recommendation would be a tomato zucchini sauce, infused with Italian herbs. Enjoy!

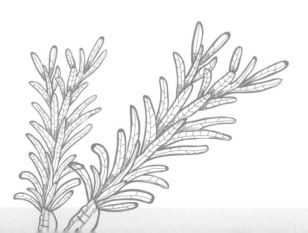

Quark Omelet Wrap

Who says omelets are just for breakfast?
This omelet is great for any time of the day.

Serves 2

INGREDIENTS:

1 cup Quark
2 eggs
3 leaves of basil
Chives
Cilantro
1 tomato – chopped
Salt and pepper
Cooking spray or coconut oil

Mix the Quark with the herbs and tomatoes in a bowl. In a separate bowl, whisk the eggs with the salt and pepper. Heat your oven to 350 degrees Fahrenheit and use a big pan for the omelet. Pour the mixture into a big pan and fry till golden. Remove the omelet, spread the Quark-Mix on top and roll the omelet like a wrap.

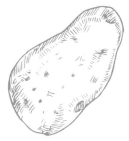

Potato Quark Strudel

Strudels, the famous Austrian dishes can be made sweet or savory.
This savory way is simply delicious!

Serves 6

INGREDIENTS:
1 lb. floury potatoes
1 cup Quark
Salt
Pepper
3 tablespoons unsalted butter
1/2 leek, thinly sliced
1 yellow pepper, diced
1 onion, peeled and diced
Zest of lemon (organic if possible) mixed with 1/2 cup of flour
1 large egg and 1 egg yolk
2 sheets of prepared strudel dough or Fillo dough sheet
(do not use puff pastry dough)

Preheat your oven to 390 degrees Fahrenheit. Bring a large pot of salted water to boil. Add the cubed potatoes and cook until tender, about 15 minutes. Drain and return the cubed potatoes to the pot. Mash potatoes with a fork. Mix in the Quark until well combined, add salt and pepper to taste. Set aside.

Heat a tablespoon of butter or oil in a skillet. Add the leek, pepper and onion and sauté, stirring, until glossy about 10 minutes. Turn off the heat. Mix the egg into the potatoes and then the leek mixture. Combine well.

Unfold one dough sheet on a damp towel. Brush with some of the remaining melted butter. Unfold the second sheet over the first and, again, brush with the rest of the melted butter. Spread the potatoes over the second sheet evenly, leaving room at the edge of the dough. Do not overfill - leftover mashed potatoes are delicious

if fried into croquettes the next day. Using the damp towel to assist you, gently lift one edge of the strudel and begin rolling it over the filling. "Glue" the edges to the side of the roll and arrange the strudel, seam-side down, on a baking sheet fitted with parchment paper. Beat the egg yolk and brush the strudel thoroughly with the egg yolk.

Bake the strudel for 40 minutes, until the strudel pastry is shiny, golden brown and crackling. Remove it from the oven, setting the pan on a cooling rack. Slice into thick pieces and serve immediately, with a green salad.

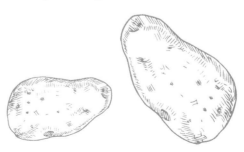

Swiss Quark Rosti

Indulge in the original taste of beautiful Switzerland, slightly modified
for Vegetarians or people looking for a low carb lunch or dinner dish.

Serves 4

INGREDIENTS:

3 ounces Quark
6 tablespoons sparkling water
6 cherry tomatoes
Salt
Pepper
1 zucchini (about 5 oz.)
2 large potatoes (each about 5 oz.)
1 tablespoon olive oil
1 bunch chives

Mix the Quark and sparkling water in a bowl until smooth. Rinse and drain the
tomatoes, cut into quarters, cut out stem ends and remove the seeds. Finely chop
tomato pulp and stir into the Quark. Season with salt and pepper. Peel zucchini
and potatoes. Grate zucchini and potatoes on a box grater. Squeeze portions firmly,
collecting liquid in a bowl. Let stand until the potato starch settles to the bottom,
1-2 minutes. Pour off liquid and mix starch with the grated vegetables.

Heat the oil in a large non-stick pan. Season vegetables with salt and pepper.
Use a tablespoon to scoop grated vegetables into pan, making 6 small Rosti. Slightly
flatten in the pan with a spatula. Cook over medium heat until crispy, about 3 minutes
on each side. Meanwhile, rinse chives, shake dry and cut into thin rings. Serve
Rosti with Quark mixture and chives.

Entrees and Quiches

The good thing about cooking with Quark is that Quark dishes will keep you full for hours and are usually low in fat. This makes it a perfect ingredient for cooking. Some of the dishes made with Quark have become really famous in different countries, like the Quiche, in Lorraine, France.

Turkey Breast with Quark Stuffing

Serves 4

INGREDIENTS:
4 thick cuts of turkey breast
1/2 cup Quark
2 slices of ham
1 tablespoon breadcrumbs
2 tablespoons chopped parsley
Salt and pepper
Vegetable oil

Preheat oven to 350 degrees Fahrenheit. Dice ham into small pieces. Put the ham into a bowl together with Quark, breadcrumbs and parsley. Mix thoroughly and season to taste with salt and pepper.

Cut deep pockets into the sides of the turkey breast filets and fill with stuffing. Add salt and pepper to the meat and fry in oil, quickly, on both sides. Put meat into a casserole. If some stuffing is left over, you can put it on top of the meat. Cook in the oven for about 10-15 minutes or the meat is thoroughly cooked.

Chicken in Cilantro Lime Sauce

This is a Mexican-inspired recipe, tasty for any occasion.

Serves 6

INGREDIENTS:
6 chicken breasts, boneless and skinless
3 tablespoons olive oil
1/4 teaspoon salt
Fresh pepper
1 teaspoon of coconut oil
For the sauce:
1 cup chicken broth (low sodium if possible)
1 teaspoon honey
1 teaspoon fresh chilli, chopped
1 cup Quark
2 cloves garlic, minced
1 teaspoon mustard (medium sharp)
2 tablespoons fresh cilantro, washed and chopped

To prepare the chicken, pour the olive oil in a large nonstick skillet. Season the chicken breasts with salt and pepper, place in skillet and let marinate for 45 minutes. Then place chicken in pan with heated coconut oil and brown them from both sides until golden and cooked through. Set aside and prepare the following sauce in a separate bowl. Mix the broth, garlic, chilli, mustard and cilantro and stir until smooth. Pour half of the sauce into your skillet, heat and then add the chicken. Turn over and cover it with rest of the sauce. Let simmer for 12-15 minutes and then reduce heat. Add the Quark and mix thoroughly. Serve immediately, preferably with brown rice, noodles and vegetables or salad. Enjoy!

Asian Pineapple Cashew-Curry

Did you know that curry powder is believed to be good for your brain, boost memory and offer protection against Alzheimer disease? No wonder it has been cherished and used since ancient times for healing. And, it pairs extremely well with the mild taste of Quark.

Serves 4-6

INGREDIENTS:

2 tablespoons curry powder
4 tablespoons butter
1 1/2 cups onion chopped
2 tablespoons flour
1/2 teaspoon fresh or ground ginger
1 cup Quark
2 cups chicken broth
1 can pineapple pieces ((preferably unsweetened)
3 cups turkey, beef or chicken (cooked, diced)
2 tablespoons lemon juice
2 tablespoons cashews
2 cups rice

Heat curry powder and butter in a large skillet. Add chopped onions and ginger, stirring frequently, until onions are softened. Blend in the flour; add chicken broth and pineapples. Bring to a boil and let the sauce cool down. Add the Quark and heat slowly (do not bring to a boil to avoid curdling). Stir in the turkey and cover for another 10 minutes. Stir in the lemon juice and serve over hot cooked rice.

Quark Quiche

This one will bring a new, enjoyable twist to the classic Quiche.
A great appetizer or lunch.

Serves 8

INGREDIENTS:

1 packet puff pastry dough (to be found in the supermarket's cooling section)
1 leek, washed and chopped
1 cup Quark
5-6 ounces (approx. 4 slices) ham
2 eggs
Salt and pepper
2 tablespoons grated cheese

Lay out the puff pastry dough onto a baking sheet or a flat quiche pan. Dice the ham and mix with Quark, eggs, leek and cheese. Season with salt and pepper using the salt sparingly, as the ham is already salty. Spread the mix on top of the dough and bake the quiche for about 30-35 minutes at 390 degrees Fahrenheit.

TIP FROM THE QUEEN
In combination with a salad, this is a well-balanced meal – wholesome and healthy!

Quiche Lorraine

Cook once, eat twice! This French Favorite can be reheated and is always a good choice for a quick or healthy snack or light meal.

Serves 6-8

IINGREDIENTS:

1 ready-to-go refrigerated pie crust or pie crust Mix (e.g. by Betty Crocker)
2 tablespoons of Quark
3 eggs
1 onion, thinly sliced
2 tomatoes, thinly sliced
4 slices of bacon (could be left out if you want to create a vegetarian friendly quiche)
1/4 teaspoon salt
Ground pepper

Heat oven to 425 degrees Fahrenheit. In a bowl, whisk the eggs and add the Quark. Mix in the other ingredients and place the mixture on the crust. Bake for 30-40 minutes and add a side salad to ensure that so you get your vitamins for the rest of the day. Bon Appetit!

Firecracker Meatballs with Herb Quark

If you love meatballs and love spicy, then this is the perfect recipe!

Makes about 30 meatballs

INGREDIENTS:

For the meatballs:
1 lb. minced meat, preferably beef
3 medium onions
2 pieces red chili
8 toast slices
4 eggs
1 1/2 teaspoon salt
½ teaspoon pepper
3 tablespoons sambal oelek
3 tablespoons oil

For the Quark Dip:
1/2 bunch parsley
1/2 bunch basil
1/2 bunch chives
1 1/4 cups Quark
3/4 cup
1/4 teaspoon salt
1/4 teaspoon pepper
2 teaspoon lemon juice

Finely chop the onions and chilies. Cut off and discard the toast crust and mix remaining toast with minced meat, onions, chilies, eggs, salt, pepper and sambal oelek. Shape into 40 small meatballs. Fry the meatballs on each side for 2 minutes. For the Quark dip, chop the parsley and basil. Cut the chives and mix the herbs with Quark, salt, pepper and lemon juice. Season to your personal taste and enjoy!

Guilt-Free Desserts

Desserts don't have to live up to their bad reputation. They can be delicious, luscious and extremely satisfying. Quark and desserts are a great combination, and the possibilities with Quark are endless. Regardless if your indulgence is ice cream, cookies or cheesecakes, Quark is the master of low-fat smoothness and it is calcium-rich as well. Here are a few mouthwatering desserts that are low in fat and sugar, pure guilt-free delights that make you feel good about your dessert choice.

Bavarian Quark Thaler

This is a lovely dessert, which originatied in
the beautiful landscape of Bavaria.

Makes 10 pieces

~~~~~~

INGREDIENTS:
2 eggs
1/4 cup milk
1/4 cup sugar
0.7 ounces yeast
2 3/4 cups flour
1/2 cup soft butter
1 pinch salt
1/2 lemon zest
1/4 sugar
1 3/4 cups quark
1 1/4 tablespoon oil
2 teaspoon cornstarch

~~~~~~

For the dough: Mix the eggs, milk, sugar and yeast for about 2 minutes. Add flour, butter, salt and knead thoroughly. Let the dough rest in a warm spot for about one hour.

For the filling: Mix the Quark, oil, cornstarch, lemon zest and sugar in a separate bowl. Separate the dough into 10 balls and flatten them on a floured worktop (about 4 inches round per thaler). The sides should be 1/2 inch higher than the middle. Place them on one or two baking papers and spoon the filling into each tahler. Let the thaler rest like this for about 30 minutes. Preheat the oven to 360 degrees Fahrenheit and bake the thaler for 15-20 minutes until they have a nice golden brown color.

   PS: Feel free to add some canned fruits like mandarin, peach etc. Just cut and put them in the middle of the thaler and put the quark filling on top.

Apricot Dumplings

Baking with Quark is baking with a passion for wellbeing.
This apricot dumpling recipe shows how good nutrition and
pure pleasure can be combined.

Makes 10 dumplings

~~~~~~

INGREDIENTS:
1 1/4 cups Quark
2 cups flour
1/4 cup butter, at room temperature
1 tablespoons vanilla powder or 1 packet vanilla sugar
1 egg
A pinch of salt
Approx. 10 small apricots
Approx. 10 sugar cubes
For the garnish:
Approx. 2 to 4 cups breadcrumbs
Approx. 1/2 cup butter
Cinnamon powder
Icing sugar

~~~~~~

Mix the softened butter with the vanilla and a small pinch of salt until creamy. Stir in the egg, the Quark and flour and work into a malleable dough. Form into a ball, wrap in film and leave in a cool place to rest for approx. 30 minutes.

Remove the stones from the apricots and replace with a sugar cube. On a floured work surface shape the dough into a roll of approx. 2.5 inches of thickness. Cut off slices and gently press these flat between the hands. Place the apricot into the dough, press the dough around it and seal well. Apply some flour to the hands, form dumplings and place on a similarly-floured board.

Bring a generous amount of slightly-salted water to a boil in a large saucepan. Turn down the heat, place the apricot dumplings in the water and allow them to simmer gently for 10–13 minutes. Stir carefully from time to time to prevent the dumplings from sticking to one another.

For the garnish, melt the butter in a pan. Add the breadcrumbs, flavor with cinnamon and fry until golden yellow in color. Use low and gentle heat. Towards the end, add a generous quantity of sugar. Carefully remove the cooked dumplings and drain well before rolling in the prepared sugared breadcrumbs. Arrange and dust with icing sugar. Serve hot. Enjoy!

TIP FROM THE QUEEN
To ensure that the dumplings do not fall apart, it is advisable to cook a test dumpling before filling with the fruit. If necessary, adjust the dough mix by adding more flour if too soft or by adding butter if too firm.

Quark Fudge Balls

This famous European desert is for anyone with a bit of
sweet tooth looking for guilt-free pleasures.

Serves 6

INGREDIENTS:
1 tablespoons cocoa powder
2/3 cup oats
1/4 cup Quark
1 teaspoon sweetener

Mix all ingredients together, saving some cocoa powder to roll the balls in later.
Roll the mixture into 1 inch balls. Roll the balls in the remaining cocoa powder.
Place the balls in the refrigerator for 15 minutes.

**TIP FROM
THE QUEEN**
*Dip your hands in
water between rolling
the balls, to keep your
palms from getting
sticky. Enjoy!*

Quark Rice Pudding

Here's a recipe for a perfect protein packed, all vegetarian desert for a delightful family dinner.

Serves 4

INGREDIENTS:
4 1/4 cups milk
1 1/4 cups rice
3 eggs
1 1/8 cups Quark
3/4 cup raspberry or strawberries
1 pear
1/8 cup butter

Bring the milk to a mild boil, reduce to medium heat, add the rice and cook for 30 minutes stirring frequently to avoid boiling over. Preheat oven to 360 degrees Fahrenheit. Beat the sugar and the eggs in a large mixing bowl until fluffy. Add and milk mixture with the Quark and stir until well mixed. Pour the quark-rice mix into the casserole dish. Cut the pear into small pieces folding the pear pieces in together with the berries. Make small butter flakes and spread them over the quark-rice mix. Bake for 40 minutes. Let it cool off and enjoy! Best when eaten while it's a still bit warm.

Vanilla Berry Quark Ice Cream

Here's an indulging, low-fat ice cream that can be made in your home kitchen without using refined sugar. Easy to make, delicious to eat!

Serves 2

INGREDIENTS:

1 cup mixed frozen berries
3/4 cup fresh Quark
1 cup vanilla Quark
2 tablespoon vanilla essence
1 tablespoon Arrowroot powder
1 teaspoon honey

Add everything except the arrowroot to a food processor and blend until completely smooth. Then mix the arrowroot powder with some water, add to mixture and blend again. You will probably have to scrape down the sides once or twice. Then transfer the mixture into a bowl, cover it and place into a freezer for an hour. Mix again, refreeze, and after another 45 minutes, enjoy!

TIP FROM THE QUEEN
All of these ice creams can be made without an ice cream machine.

Quark-Blueberry Ice Cream

With Quark ice cream you do not need to deprive yourself of getting
a second portion. This Blueberry Ice Cream is super easy
to make at home and is – as all the Quark Fruit Ice creams –
high in protein, vitamins, calcium, and low in fat.

Serves 2

INGREDIENTS:
1 1/4 cups Quark
1 tablespoon honey
1 cup frozen blueberries
1/2 cup soy, almond or low fat milk

Combine the ingredients in a mixer and mix them well. Fill mixture into 2 bowls
and place them in the freezer until it has an icy texture. Decorate with fresh fruit
and enjoy!

Famous Cheesecakes

Baking with Quark has many advantages. First, you automatically increase the protein content of the cake. Second, it allows you to reduce the amount of fat and other ingredients such as flour. The difference between Quark-cheesecake and the classic cheesecake is obvious: Quark-cheesecake contains less than half the amount of cholesterol and fat as its classic names cake made with cream cheese. Now you can have your cheesecake and eat it too!

Mango Cheesecake

Serves 4

INGREDIENTS:

1 1/4 cups Quark
1/3 cup sugar or sweetener
3 eggs
3.5 ounces fresh or frozen mango, peeled and chopped
5 tablespoons butter
3.5 ounces chocolate chip cookies, crushed
3 tablespoons low fat yoghurt
2 tablespoons coconut flakes

For the topping: Mix Quark, sugar, mangoes and eggs together. Add yoghurt and resist the temptation of eating it right away. Set aside.

For the base: melt the butter and mix the crushed cookies in. Then pour the topping mixture into the baking pan till the entire base is covered. Bake for one hour and remove the cake after it has cooled. Decorate with coconut flakes and fruits, such as blueberries or raspberries.

Crumble Poppy Quark Cake

Try this easy recipe and fall in love with its sweet tanginess, as usual
with Quark: Powered by protein, calcium and magnesium!

Serves 6

INGREDIENTS:

1 cup poppy seeds, ground
1/2 cup sugar
1 3/4 cups milk
1/2 cup semolina
1 egg
For the shortcrust:
1/2 cup butter, unsalted, cold
3/4 cup powdered sugar
2 1/4 cups flour
1 tablespoon vanilla powder or the pulp of 1 Vanilla bean
For the Quark filling:
3 eggs
1/2 cup butter, unsalted, soft
1/3 cup cornstarch
1 cup sugar
2 tablespoons vanilla powder or the pulp of 2 Vanilla bean
1 pinch salt
1 1/2 cups Quark

Place the poppy seeds, sugar, milk, semolina, butter and egg in a pot and bring
to a boil. Turn off the heat and let it cool. Place the baking paper on your spring
form pan and grease the frame with coconut oil or butter. Then preheat the oven to
360 degrees Fahrenheit.

For the crust: Combine powdered sugar, flour, butter and vanilla and knead it well. Divide the dough into half and let one half cool in the refrigerator. Press the other half into the bottom of your pan, leave the sides free.

For the filling: Beat the eggs, butter and cornstarch until light and fluffy. Then continue by adding sugar, vanilla, salt and Quark. First add poppy seed filling, then quark filling on the dough bottom. Crumble the remaining cooled dough over the Quark filling. Bake for 1 hour, if necessary, cover after about 30 minutes with aluminum foil to prevent the top from getting too dark. Turn off the oven and let the cake rest for 10 minutes. Remove from oven, let it cool on a wire rack for 2 hours, and then chill in refrigerator for 3 hours, or even better over night.

Low Fat German Cheesecake

Famous in Germany – beloved around the world and not just because
of its low fat content, but because it is simply divine!

Serves 6

～～～～～～～～～～～～～～～～～～～～～～～～～～

18 ounces Quark
3 large eggs
1 3/4 cup sugar or 1/2 cup stevia for less calories
4.5 ounces Butter
2 packs vanilla sugar
2 tablespoons semolina
1 teaspoon baking powder
1 pack vanilla pudding mix
the juice of 1 lemon

～～～～～～～～～～～～～～～～～～～～～～～～～～

Blend sugar, eggs and butter in a large bowl with an electric mixer until smooth.
Add, and mix Quark, vanilla sugar and semolina. Then stir in vanilla pudding mix.
Pour filling into a round, buttered cake pan. Bake for 180 minutes at 390 degrees
Fahrenheit. Turn off the oven and let it rest for 30 minutes with an open door.
Enjoy when it is still warm. DELICIOUS!

Pumpkin Cheesecake with Cinnamon Crumbles

With this lip-smacking goodness you can indulge in the luscious taste of pumpkins and cinnamon. Perfect in the fall or for any festive season.

Serves 4

INGREDIENTS:

For the dough:
5 tablespoons sugar
1 teaspoon cinnamon
3 cups flour
1 teaspoon baking powder
1/4 teaspoon salt
2/3 cup butter, soft
1 egg yolk

For the filling:
1 cup pumpkin, cooked
1 1/4 cups Quark
1 cup creme fraiche
1/3 cup sugar
2 eggs
1/4 cup lemon juice
Zest of lemons
1/4 cup cornstarch

Heat the oven to 360°degrees Fahrenheit. Line a 10 inch cake pan with baking parchment. Grease the walls of the cake pan. Knead the ingredients from the dough until you get crumbles. For the bottom, put half of the dough into the spring form pan and press in firmly by hand. Use a fork to make a few holes into the dough.

Bake for 15-20 minutes and then let it cool for 15 minutes. Puree the pumpkin and mix it together with the remaining ingredients for the filling. Pour it on the baked bottom and cover with the remaining cinnamon crumbles. Bake for 45 minutes, cover it with aluminum foil, reduce heat to 300 degrees Fahrenheit and continue baking for another 50 minutes. Cool and enjoy!

Lemon Cheesecake

This is a recipe for a culinary citrus flavored pleasure
that is simply guilt-free!

Serves 4

INGREDIENTS:

For the crust:
1 1/2 cups digestive cookie crumbs or graham crackers,
about 14 cookies, finely crushed
6 tablespoons unsalted butter, melted, plus more for greasing
2 tablespoons sugar
1/4 teaspoon fine sea salt
For the filling:
3 eggs, separated
3/4 cup sugar
1 teaspoon vanilla extract
1/4 teaspoon almond extract
1 Tonka bean, finely grated (optional) or 1 generous pinch ground cardamom
6 tablespoons unsalted butter, softened
2 1/2 cups Quark
Zest of 3 lemons, plus extra for garnish
1 1/2 tablespoons cornstarch
Generous pinch of fine sea salt
Powdered sugar, for garnish
1/2 lemon, sliced into 1/2-inch slivers, then cut in half to form triangles
Fresh lemon juice, for garnish

Line an 8x8-inch square pan with parchment paper, and generously grease the paper with a little melted butter. Pulse digestive cookies in a food processor until finely ground. Add butter, sugar, and salt and pulse a few more times until

well-blended. Press mixture evenly into lined pan. Bake at 350 degrees Fahrenheit for 10 to 12 minutes or until golden-brown.

Preheat oven to 325 degrees Fahrenheit. In a separate bowl, beat the egg yolks and sugar for about 2 to 3 minutes on high speed until pale yellow. Add vanilla, almond extract, Tonka bean (if using) or ground cardamom, and softened butter until combined. Add the Quark, lemon zest, cornstarch, and salt and then mix until thoroughly combined.

In a large, clean metal bowl, whisk the egg whites until stiff peaks form. Gently fold egg whites into egg yolk/quark filling. Pour into the prepared pan with crust and bake on a sheet pan for about 1 hour, until golden. The center will still be a little wobbly. Turn oven off and allow to sit cooling in the oven for 10 minutes. Remove from oven, cool for about an hour on a wire rack, and refrigerate for at least 2 hours before removing from pan and serving. It will sink and settle a bit as it cools — it's supposed to do that! Cake can be made up to 1 day in advance.

When ready to serve, remove from pan and cut into 1-inch squares (or larger if you prefer). Top each square with a small, triangular lemon slice, extra lemon zest, a squeeze of lemon juice and a bit of powdered sugar.

Cookies, Muffins and Pies

Cookie Lovers will appreciate the following really tasty recipes that are heavenly but light, since they are not loaded with extra fat and calories unlike many traditional cookies. Quark works perfectly for baking and ensures homemade culinary pleasures.

Rhubarb and Lime Muffins

Makes 12 Muffins

INGREDIENTS:

9 ounces rhubarb
4 ounces cane sugar
1 lime
½ vanilla bean
¾ cup milk (low-fat)
2 ounces cultured butter
4 ounces spelt semolina
2 eggs
1 pinch salt
4 ounces Quark

Rinse rhubarb, drain, trim and cut into approximately 1/4-inch thick slices. Mix rhubarb in a bowl with approximately 2 tablespoons sugar and let stand for 10 minutes. Meanwhile rinse lime in hot water, dry, grate peel finely and mix zest with rhubarb. Cut vanilla bean lengthwise, scrape out seeds, add to a small pot and bring to a boil with milk and butter. Sprinkle spelt semolina into pot and bring to a boil, stirring constantly with a wooden spoon. Separate eggs. In a high vessel, beat egg whites with a hand mixer, add a pinch of salt, and beat until stiff. Gradually add approximately 1/4 cup sugar and continue to beat until sugar dissolves. Mix quark, egg yolks and rhubarb into warm spelt batter, then fold in egg whites. Line a 12-cup muffin tin with paper baking cups. Pour batter into cups and sprinkle with remaining sugar. Bake in preheated oven at approximately 400 degrees Fahrenheit/convection 350 degrees Fahrenheit, on middle oven rack for about 25 minutes. Remove tin from oven and let cool for 5 minutes. Then remove muffins from tin and let cool completely on a wire rack for about 1 hour before serving.

Cinnamon Apple Muffin

"An apple a day keeps the doctor away." This recipe brings back sweet childhood memories and the smell of my grandmother's cozy kitchen.

12 Muffins

INGREDIENTS:
3 ounces of soft butter (2/3 sticks)
1/4 cup sugar
1/2 teaspoon vanilla powder or the pulp of half a vanilla pod
2 eggs
2 cups Quark
1/2 cup flour
2 teaspoons baking powder
1 middle-sized apple
2 tablespoons chopped walnuts

Mix butter and sugar, then add eggs and Quark, and stir to a soft batter. Mix flour and baking powder, then add to the batter. Cut the apple, remove the core and dice finely. Stir walnuts and apple pieces into the batter. Fill batter into the molds of a muffin pan and bake in the preheated oven at 390 degrees Fahrenheit for 25-30 minutes until the muffins are golden-brown.

TIP FROM THE QUEEN
Use genuine vanilla (out of the pod) instead of artificial vanilla flavor to make use of nature's superpowers whenever possible. The vanilla pod – queen of spices – has many healing properties which help to sustain your body!

Cheesecake Muffins with Blueberries

Meet the Austrian version of the Queen of Muffins, combining the superfood powers of blueberries with the heavenly taste of cheesecake.

12 Muffins

INGREDIENTS:
1 cup fresh blueberries
3/4 cup butter
7/8 cup sugar
4 eggs
5.3 ounces Quark
8.8 ounces cream cheese
1 generous pinch vanilla-bean seed
1 generous pinch grated lemon peel (untreated)
1 pinch salt
2 1/4 tablespoons cornstarch
1 teaspoon baking powder
powdered sugar (for dusting)

Preheat the oven to 350 degrees Fahrenheit. Line the wells of a muffin tin with paper liners. Rinse berries and drain on paper towels. Beat butter with sugar until creamy and whisk in the eggs gradually. Stir in the Quark, cream cheese, vanilla, lemon zest and salt. Mix cornstarch with the baking powder and stir in. Pour half of the batter into the muffin wells, add about 80 grams (approx. 3 oz) to 3/4 cup of berries and cover with the remaining batter. Bake in preheated oven until golden brown, about 30 minutes. If muffins start to become too dark, cover with aluminum foil. Remove from oven, let cool slightly, release from the tin and let cool on a wire rack. Top with the remaining berries and serve dusted with powdered sugar.

The Quark Kaiserschmarrn — Delectably delicious!

A truly famous European and especially Austrian pastry! Originally it is called Quark Schmarren and is eaten as a dessert.

Serves 2

~~~~~~

INGREDIENTS:

1 ounce golden raisins or cranberries
3 tablespoons rum, white wine or apple juice
3 eggs
1 vanilla pod
5 ounces Quark
4 ounces pastry flour
1/4 cup milk (low-fat)
2 1/4 tablespoons sugar
2 tablespoons butter

~~~~~~

In a small pot, bring the raisins and wine or rum or apple juice, whatever you have chosen to a boil. Remove from heat and let it cool. Separate the eggs. Split the vanilla pod lengthwise and scrape out the seeds with a sharp knife. Mix together the yolks, vanilla seeds, quark, flour, milk and cane sugar until well combined. Beat egg whites to very stiff peaks and gently fold the egg whites into the Quark mixture. Transfer the batter to a buttered, oven-proof pan and heat over medium heat until thickened. Drain the raisins, discard the liquid and sprinkle the raisins over the batter. Bake in a preheated oven at 360 degrees Fahrenheit until set, about 15-20 minutes. Tear the finished pancake into pieces with two forks and divide among plates. Sprinkle with a little bit of powdered sugar, if desired, and serve warm. Enjoy!

Chocolate Chip Quark Cookies

Makes 18-24 cookies

INGREDIENTS:

1 cup unsalted butter, softened to room temperature
1/2 cup Quark
1 cup sugar
2 eggs
1 teaspoon vanilla extract
3 1/2 cups all-purpose flour
1 teaspoon fresh lemon juice
1 teaspoon cornstarch
1 teaspoon baking soda
1/2 teaspoon salt
2 cups semisweet chocolate chunks or chocolate chips, divided

Preheat oven to 350 degrees Fahrenheit. Line cookie sheets with parchment paper and set aside. Blend butter and Quark until creamed. Add sugar and lemon. Blend until light and fluffy. Add eggs, continue mixing and stir in vanilla extract. In a separate, medium-sized bowl whisk together flour, salt, cornstarch and baking soda. Continue mixing and gradually add all the flour mixture to your dough. Stir in ¾ of the chocolate chunks until they are well incorporated. Use 2 tablespoons to scoop dough onto baking parchment and use hands if necessary to roll the dough. Set the balls of dough at least 2 apart, and bake for 10 minutes. When coming out of the oven, gently press remaining chocolate chunks into the tops of each cookie. Allow cookies to cool on baking sheet for at least 10 minutes and enjoy warm.

Quark Biscuits with Jam

Biscuits are simply lovely with tea or coffee! Learn from the British aristocracy where they are called scones and enjoy your biscuits at tea time, which usually takes place between 3 and 5 pm.

Makes 10-15 biscuits

INGREDIENTS:

2 cups all-purpose flour
2 tablespoons sugar
2 teaspoons baking powder
1 teaspoon salt
1 cup Quark
3 teaspoons jam , e.g. raspberry, orange or strawberry
2/3 cup water

Preheat oven to 450 degrees Fahrenheit. Sift flour, sugar, baking powder and salt into a large bowl. Whisk Quark and water in a small bowl. Make a well in the dry ingredients. Add Quark mixture and stir with a fork until just blended. Do not over-mix.

Turn the dough out onto a lightly floured surface. Knead a few times and pat into a 1-inch-thick circle. Cut out biscuits with a floured 2- ½-inch round cutter and place on an ungreased baking sheet. Press dough scraps together and repeat to make 12 biscuits in all. Bake until tops are golden and firm to the touch, 12-15 minutes. Serve warm and enjoy! It's teatime.

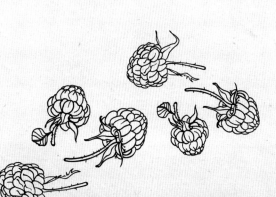

Red Fruit Pie

Fruits are a gateway to vitality. You can enjoy this fruit pie
at any time and feel entirely guilt-free.

Serves 6

INGREDIENTS:
2 cups flour
1/3 tablespoons sugar
1 pinch salt
7 tablespoons butter (room temperature)
1 egg yolk
2 tablespoons cold water
2 1/4 cups cream Quark
2 teaspoons vanilla sugar
3 tablespoons sugar
2 eggs
1 cup frozen blueberries and raspberries (can be replaced by other frozen fruit)

Mix the all-purpose flour with a pinch of salt and the sugar. Cut the butter into small cubes and add the butter cubes one at a time to the flour mixture. Continue mixing gently with the flat beater attachment if you have one or with a fork until all the butter has been added. Keep on mixing until the mixture looks crumbly. Add the egg yolk and cold water. Keep on mixing until a dough ball has formed. Wrap the dough in cling film and let it rest in the refrigerator for about 1 hour.

Preheat the oven to 180 degrees Fahrenheit. Coat the pie form with butter. Add a little bit of flour to the countertop and use a rolling-pin to roll out the dough. Press the dough into the cake pan and poke holes in the bottom using a fork. In a separate bowl create a smooth mixture of Quark, eggs, vanilla sugar and 1 tablespoon of sugar. Divide the mixture over the bottom and divide the fruit over the filling. Divide another 2 tablespoons over the fruit. Bake the pie in the oven for about 40 minutes, or until it's a beautiful golden brown. Let it cool off a bit and serve warm or cold.

Blueberry Quark Squares

This makes a wonderful afternoon snack for the kids or for the whole family and friends.

Makes 16 pieces

INGREDIENTS:
2 2/3 cups flour
3 1/3 tablespoons of yeast
1/3 cup sugar
7/8 cup milk
1 cup almond flour
1 egg
1 teaspoon grated lemon peel
1 pinch salt
1/3 cup soft butter
flour (for working)
Filling:
5 1/3 cups blueberries
1 1/3 cups Quark
7/8 cup créme fraiche
2 eggs
1 tablespoon corn starch
1/2 cup sugar
1/2 cup almonds (roughly chopped)
2 tablespoons candied lemon peel (roughly chopped)
1 generous pinch cinnamon
Crumble:
2 cups flour
7/8 cup sugar
7/8 cup butter

For the pastry, put the flour in a heap on a work surface and make a well in the center. Crumble the yeast into the well and mix with 1 teaspoon sugar, a little lukewarm milk and a little of the flour. Cover and let stand for about 20 minutes to allow the yeast to start working. Then add the rest of the sugar, the ground almonds, lemon peel, salt, butter and egg and combine with the flour, working the ingredients together from the center outwards. Gradually add the rest of the milk. Knead well and let rise again for 30 minutes. Wash and drain the blueberries and preheat the oven to 350 degrees Fahrenheit. Roll out the pastry on a floured work surface and lay on a cookie sheet lined with baking parchment, forming a raised edge about 1 inch high. Prick the base several times with a fork. For the filling, mix the Quark, creme fraiche, eggs, cornstarch, sugar, chopped almonds, candied peel and cinnamon and spread on the pastry. Scatter with blueberries. For the crumble, rub the flour, sugar and butter between your hands or in a bowl to produce a crumbly consistency and scatter on top of the blueberries. Bake in the preheated oven (middle shelf) for about 30 minutes until the pastry is nicely browned. Cut into pieces before serving.

Nutritious Breads

Baking with Quark is ideal. It adds creaminess as well as protein, calcium and vital minerals to your daily diet. Due to the fact that Quark contains less liquid than for example milk, you may need to add a little extra liquid to the dough by adding sparkling water or almond milk.

Quark Pita Bread

Pita bread is a delicious and very healthy replacement
for chips or tacos.

Makes 12 pieces

INGREDIENTS:

1/4 cup parmesan, grated
1 tablespoon parsley, chopped
2 garlic cloves, finely chopped or grated
1 1/2 cups mozzarella
3 tablespoons crème fraîche
1 egg
1/2 cup Quark
1/8 cup butter
2 3/4 cups flour
1 egg
1 pinch sugar
1 teaspoon salt
1 egg yolk
1 tablespoon water

Mix 1 tablespoon parmesan with the parsley and set aside. In a bowl, mix the rest of the parmesan, garlic, mozzarella, crème fraîche and egg. In another bowl knead quark, butter, flour, egg, sugar and salt. Take half the dough and roll it out on a floured surface (11inch). Transfer it onto a baking sheet. Spread the cheese-mix on it and leave about 1 inch of the edge free of the cheese mix. Roll out the other half and place it on top of the dough covered in cheese-mix. With your fingers press the dough edges together and fold it inside, so that the bread is completely sealed. Mix yolk and water and brush it onto the dough. With a knife cut a few lines into the bread. Bake for 20-25 minutes until golden-brown by 375 degrees Fahrenheit. Garnish the warm bread with the parmesan-parsley mix and enjoy!

Strawberry Banana Bread

Here's a recipe for the perfect snack containing fiber,
protein and vitamins.

Makes 1 loaf

INGREDIENTS:
1 1/2 cups whole wheat pastry flour
1 1/2 teaspoons baking powder
3 ripe bananas
1 cup fresh or frozen strawberries or cranberries
1/2 cups of almonds or walnuts
1/2 teaspoon salt
2 eggs
4 tablespoons sugar or turbinado sugar
1/2 cup organic honey
3/4 cup Quark

Preheat the oven to 375 degrees Fahrenheit. Combine the flour, baking powder and salt in a large bowl. Mash the bananas in a separate bowl using a fork and then add the sugar, eggs, honey and mix well. Add the Quark and whisk until smooth. Pour the prepared mixture onto the ingredients in the other bowl and mix well. Pour the batter into a loaf pan and bake for 35-40 minutes until the top is golden brown. Use a toothpick to check if it is ready. When it comes out clean it is done. Let it cool down before slicing.

Quark Bread

Here's a simple to prepare and very enjoyable recipe, with sweet or savory topping.

Makes 1 loaf

INGREDIENTS:

2 cups flour
2 cups Quark
2 eggs
3 teaspoons baking powder
1/4 teaspoons salt
2 ounces butter

Mix all ingredients to form a solid dough and put it into a pan lined ith baking parchment. Bake for 1 hour at 380 degrees Fahrenheit.

Quark Nut Rolls

These nut rolls are made so much lighter by using Quark
that they are a true low carb pleasure.

Makes 9 rolls

INGREDIENTS:
2 1/3 cups whole wheat flour
1 1/4 cups Quark
1 egg
1/2 teaspoon salt
4 teaspoons baking powder
1 cup hazelnuts or walnuts

Preheat the oven to 360 degrees Fahrenheit. Combine all ingredients in a bowl. Mix all ingredients using your hands or a hand mixer with dough hooks. Divide the dough into 8-9 balls and place them on baking paper on a baking sheet. Bake for 20 minutes in the oven. Cool and enjoy!

Make your own Quark

Milk, lactic acid bacteria, and vegetarian rennet (or another acid activator) – that's all you need to make your own Quark. You can buy these ingredients in retail stores, in organic grocery shops, and of course online. Rennet is sold in tablet form and as a liquid. The necessary bacteria cultures can be found in small packages in the cooling section of your local grocery store or online.

BASIC FORMULA: SIMPLE LOW-FAT QUARK WITH RENNET

¼ gallon milk (1 pt.)
1 packet trace homophilic Quark bacteria
1/2 tablet of rennet or 15 drops of liquid rennet

Dissolve the tablet in a tablespoon of water and stir into the milk together with the lactic bacteria. Place this starter in a warm environment (86 degrees Fahrenheit is ideal). Wait for the timeframe explained in the starter kit. The periods of fermentation may vary – please also read the information on the bacteria package. Normally, the fermentation is complete after roughly 10 hours which means that Quark and whey are separated. Now, line a sieve with a thin tea towel and pour the Quark into it. In order to get a soft and creamy Quark, you should not let it drip off too long, because the more liquid the Quark loses, the more solidified it becomes.

TIP FROM THE QUEEN
Gather the dripped-off whey and put it to good use – for instance with a royally delicious smoothie!

QUARK FORMULA WITH LEMON JUICE

1/4 gallon milk (1 pt.)
2 tablespoons lemon juice

Heat the milk to 86 degrees Fahrenheit. Add the lemon juice and stir well with a whisk. Cover the starter with a cloth and let it sit at room temperature for 30 minutes. During this time, solid and liquid parts will separate. Now you can drip off the Quark using a sieve lined with a thin tea towel.

TIP FROM THE QUEEN
After sieving, stir the Quark once more and either eat it right away or store it in a clean container in your refrigerator. Freshly made Quark will keep for about 2-3 days.

THE DIY AUTOMATED WAY

Also you could use a modern kitchen appliance to produce Quark, e.g the Cuisinart© CYM-100 Electronic Yogurt Maker. It will take 16 hours to produce Quark from buttermilk with it and it has an integrated automatic cooling system, wich makes things even easier. When the production process ends you can drain the Quark in the Cuisipro Donvier Yogurt Cheese Maker.

PART 3

Beauty Applications

The many healing properties of Quark are still largely unfamiliar to most Americans. Yet Quark can do wonders for your skin. Like avocados, Quark is a superfood not just in a nutritional way but also for external beauty applications. Healthy skin is essential to looking and feeling great, and many products promise rejuvenating results. The skin is a truly complex and fascinating organ, covering about 20 square feet per average adult. It provides an important barrier between the inside and the outside world. 24 hours a day the skin is healing, recovering, protecting and repairing damages that have been created by age, sun exposure or toxic influences. Quark can work miracles and helps soothe your skin and help you maintain a protective barrier against external stresses to your skin and your health. The following are external applications for your personal wellness, relaxation and skin rejuvenation.

Natural Bath Soaks

There are various ways to enjoy a healing bath with Quark or whey. Whether you opt for the pure version or decide to make use of additional components, it is always relaxing and healthy. A Quark bath is an effective therapeutic remedy. Quark pampers the skin and strengthens the metabolism. If you take your time and regard your bath as your personal R&R, it will be even better. Let some self-care with Quark add an inner smile to your outer beauty and you will feel truly royal!

Taking a Bath: Accurate for all Quark baths, no matter which additives you choose, the following description is accurate for all Quark baths. Relax and enjoy! A water temperature of 95-100 degrees Fahrenheit and a time period of 20-30 minutes are perfect. If you stretch the time a little longer – no problem. After your bath, you should rinse off the remains of the bath water under a lukewarm shower. Treat yourself to 30 minutes of rest afterwards. This way, the therapeutic effect can develop fully. Your self-healing powers are activated.

THE PURE QUARK BATH

Sometimes you just don't want special scents or other additives –
then pure Quark is just the thing.

As your bath essence, stir 2 cups of Quark into 4 cups of hot water so that it dissolves completely. Using a whisk works best. Pour the mix into your bath water. Enjoy!

THE BATH WITH QUARK AND HONEY

This combination is also very soothing.

Whisk up 1 tablespoon honey, 2 cups Quark, and 4 cups of hot water. Once the mix has dissolved well, pour it into your bath water. Relax and enjoy.

THE WHEY BATH

Whey has a lot of soothing and healing properties, too.
A whey bath refreshes the skin.

Stir 8 cups of whey into your bath water. Since the whey is cold when added, the original water temperature should be slightly higher than the necessary 95-100 degrees Fahrenheit. Otherwise, a whey bath is done exactly like a Quark bath.

TIP FROM THE QUEEN
You can add enjoyable extras to your whey bath just like you do with the Quark bath.

Foot Baths:

PURE WITH QUARK

Natural medicine teaches us that the foot mirrors the
complete person. No wonder that therapeutic treatments of the
feet will reflect positively on the whole body.

Stir 1 cup of Quark with a whisk into about 2 cups of hot water so that it dissolves
well. Add this Quark water to the foot bath you prepared. A bath temperature of
95-100 degrees Fahrenheit and a time period of 20-30 minutes are perfect. If you
take a little extra time – no problem! After the bath, you should wash your feet
with lukewarm water to rinse off the remains of the Quark water. Treat yourself to
30 minutes of rest after your foot bath so that the therapeutic effect can fully
develop. Your self-healing powers will be activated.

STIMULATING WITH QUARK AND ROSEMARY OIL

Quark is care, rosemary secures the stimulation – a wonderful mix
because of the uplifting effect when you feel tired and low-spirited.

Whisk 10 drops of rosemary oil and 1 cup of Quark into 2 cups of water until fully
dissolved. Add this mix to your foot bath.

TIP FROM THE QUEEN
*Even if this bath has a stimulating effect and you feel fit and alive after-
wards, you might want to treat yourself to 30 minutes of rest afterwards.
It will do you good!*

SOOTHING WITH QUARK AND LAVENDER OIL

Lavender calms down and soothes the soul.

Whisk 10 drops of lavender oil and 1 cup of Quark into 2 cups of water until it dissolves fully. Add this mix to your foot bath.

Hair Care with Quark

Dying, drying, constant shampooing, environmental influences –
hair has to endure a lot. Enough reason to pamper it from time to time!
Quark strengthens your hair. You can smooth out brittle hair
texture and give your hair a silky shine.

Dissolve 1 tablespoon of honey in ¼ cup lukewarm olive oil. Add the mix to 1 cup of Quark. The longer your hair, the more you will need of the mix. Wash your hair as usual and towel it dry. Now apply the Quark-oil-mix and spread it evenly over your hair. Allow a treatment time of 30 minutes, then carefully rinse out with warm water.

Soothing Massages

Massages are generally pleasant and relaxing - a feast for body and soul. With the matching massage product, this effect will be enhanced by far.

Even though it is possible to massage many regions of your body yourself, it might be worth the luxury not to. The pleasure of relaxing becomes so much greater when you can just lie down and let someone else treat you. It's so much fun and so good for your health at the same time!

MASSAGE WITH QUARK-OIL

To give the Quark more elasticity, mix it with a little oil so that it can be more easily spread on the skin. The effects of oil and Quark complement each other; use a high-quality oil, it is worth it. The Quark-Oil-Massage will loosen up tight muscles, help you relax, and care for your skin at the same time. It will be a rejuvenating treatment.

Add one tablespoon of oil per ½ cup of Quark. Olive oil, almond oil, avocado oil or argan oil are ideal. The amount you need depends on the body region you want to massage.

TIP FROM THE QUEEN
If you have some of the mix left over, it will keep in the refrigerator for 2-3 days.

And this is how it's done: Warm up the Quark-oil-mix in your hands and then spread it on the skin. Carry out the massage with slow movements and medium to strong pressure, applying the mix generously. You can alternate between stroking, kneading, and tapping on the skin. The massage should last at least 15 minutes but might also take up to 30 minutes. For the receiving person, it will feel like a mini-wellness-trip. Afterwards, the Quark is rinsed off with warm water. Just like with the baths, it is useful to rest after the massage to give the power of Quark time to work.

TAPPING MASSAGE WITH QUARK AND WHEY

In Ayurveda, the tapping massage with little herb bags is popular.
This kind of massage will also work with Quark. The soft tapping
helps to let the skin absorb the active substances so that
they can work their magic there.

You need two handkerchiefs or other pieces of cotton, approximatcly the size of a kitchen towel. In fact you can use two kitchen towels.

Bring 1/8 lb. of rice to a boil in ½ cup of whey. Then let the rice simmer at low temperature until it is done. It is ready when the liquid has completely vanished. Let it cool for a while, then add 4 tablespoons of Quark. This warm (but not hot!) mix is ladled into the middle of the cotton cloths. Pull up the corners so that little bags are formed which you can hold.

This is how it's done: Take the little bags with the rice in your hands and massage the chosen body region by steadily tapping it. Alternate the intensity of the tapping between gentle and strong – it should always feel nice, though. This tapping is a very pleasing technique for the face and the décolleté area.

TIP FROM THE QUEEN
By adding naturally active oils, you can even include a whiff of aroma-therapy. Lavender is soothing, orange lifts the mood, and rosemary is stimulating.

Compresses and Poultices

In Europe, many people remember this application from their childhood days. Many grandmothers have lovingly taken care of smaller and sometimes bigger ailments of their grandchildren this way. Nowadays, these treasure troves of natural medicine are finally making a comeback.

Compresses and poultices with Quark can be used in many different cases: with coughs, skin rashes, insect stings, or sprains.

When the Quark turns dry on the skin, there might be a feeling of tightness. This is okay and even desired. The skin metabolism is enhanced which is a good thing.

Very rarely do Quark poultices cause skin irritation. If you belong to the few people who experience an uneasy feeling when Quark touches their skin, you can apply Quark on top of a tea towel and as such, forego direct skin contact. Of course, the effect will be somewhat weakened this way.

You will need cotton cloths – tea towels work very well here - a woolen cloth or thicker towel to hold in the natural warmth, and of course Quark.

And this is how it's done: Spread Quark on the skin to about the thickness of a finger, wrap up and cover twice with the tea towels. Now swathe in the wool cloth so that it is kept warm. That's it – now you just wait. The Quark is allowed to work for about an hour. After that, the cloths are removed and the Quark is rinsed off with lukewarm water.

Facial Masks

Anti-aging measures do not have to be expensive. Quark is a true miracle worker when it comes to skin care. Everyone seeking to look refreshed and who puts an emphasis on clean skin and a nice complexion will love the Quark facial.

PURE QUARK FACIAL

The power of Quark without any artificial additives –
a fountain of youth for you!

Mix 6 tablespoons Quark with 1-2 tablespoons whey – your foundation is ready.

This is how it's done: Gently clean your face and pat dry. Now spread the Quark mix evenly and let it dry. During this half-hour you might feel a little tightness or a slight itch; that is normal and means the enzymes in the Quark are working their magic. After 30 minutes, remove the Quark mix thoroughly with warm water and pat dry again. Do not use any face cream right afterwards; the Quark still needs time to work.

TIP FROM THE QUEEN
If your skin is very dry, you can add a trace of Argan oil to the mix as an additional care factor.

FACIAL WITH QUARK AND HONEY

Quark and honey are a great combination. This facial is
particularly stimulating to the metabolism. The skin
receives a perfect detox treatment.

Stir together 6 tablespoons Quark, 1-2 tablespoons whey, and 1 tablespoon honey, until you get a creamy paste.

This is how it's done: Gently clean your face and pat dry. Now spread the Quark mix evenly and let it dry. During this half-hour you might feel a little tightness or a slight itch; that is normal and means the enzymes in the Quark are working their magic. After 30 minutes, remove the Quark mix thoroughly with warm water and pat dry again. Do not use any face cream right afterwards; Quark and honey are still at work within your skin.

FACIAL WITH QUARK AND CUCUMBER

The combination of Quark and cucumber is particularly refreshing
and rejuvenating for the skin.

Peel about a quarter of a normal-sized cucumber, cut into small pieces, and blend it in the blender. Stir it together with 6-8 tablespoons of Quark to form a creamy paste.

This is how it's done: Gently clean your face and pat dry. Now spread the Quark mix evenly and let it dry. During this half-hour you might feel a little tightness or a slight itch; that is normal and means the enzymes in the Quark are working their magic. After 30 minutes, remove the Quark mix thoroughly with warm water and pat dry again. Do not use any face cream right afterwards; the mix still needs time to work.

QUARK FACIAL WITH PEELING

The Quark facial itself already comes with a peeling effect. But you can enhance this by adding coarse sea salt or coriander seeds.

Stir together 6 tablespoons Quark with 1-2 tablespoons whey to form a creamy paste. Add 2 tablespoons coarse sea salt or coriander seeds and apply right away. Your peeling facial is ready!

This is how it's done: Gently clean your face and pat dry. Now spread the Quark mix evenly and let it dry. During this half-hour you might feel a little tightness or a slight itch; that is normal and means the enzymes in the Quark are working their magic. After 30 minutes, remove the Quark mix thoroughly with warm water and pat dry again. Now you can feel the peeling effect of the salt or the seeds. Do not use any face cream right afterwards; the Quark still needs time to work.

Rejuvenation and Anti-Aging with Quark

Who doesn't want to look beautiful and radiant? Quark is the perfect assistant! Circles under your eyes; nobody wants them. Dark circles under your eyes testify to tiredness and too much work.

The perfect mix: Stir up Quark with a shot of olive oil and a tablespoon of lemon juice. Apply this mix daily (preferably three times a week) to the skin under your eyes and let it sit for 30 minutes. Afterwards, remove gently with warm water, keeping your eyes shut. It will take a while to see the results, but it will work!

QUARK AND WRINKLES.

Wrinkles are basically lines that life drew on us. They show that we like to laugh and have shed a tear or experienced sadness here and there. While we strive for smooth and healthy skin, we encourage the acceptance of ageing. We believe in self-care, including skin care, and Quark can help your skin look and feel smoother and healthier.

The cosmetics industry makes billions with anti-wrinkle products, because everybody wants to look younger and have a smooth skin. Sometimes, this puts a lot of pressure on people, especially if a career calls for a youthful look.

A well-functioning metabolism is a prerequisite for a healthy skin. You can stimulate clean and healthy skin with a whey cure.

Quark facials applied two to four times a week have a positive effect. You can alternate between pure Quark, Quark-honey, or Quark-cucumber formulas. These facials will tighten your skin, prevent wrinkles, and improve the skin texture, even if some wrinkles are already apparent.

QUARK AND HANDS

This is a typical winter problem: the cold makes the skin rough and irritated, even to the point where the skin will even split and crack, often starting at the knuckles.

One can get relief with a daily hand bath. The application works just like a foot bath: apply Quark directly to the hands and let the moisture soak into your skin, 10-15 minutes is enough. If the problems are severe, you can complement it with a Quark poultice twice a week.

QUARK AND FEET

Who doesn't want to have pretty feet? But reality is often quite different. Sometimes the skin on one's feet and heels is dry and cracked. Sometimes this is a sign of other health problems – the thyroid, for instance, can be a cause for it. But even wearing poorly fitting shoes, or too much stress on the feet can be the culprit.

Healthy skin is beautiful, and dry skin is not just a problem of appearance. When the skin on the feet is dry and fissured, socks and stockings get caught in the cracks, which is a nuisance. But even worse: the cracks can get so deep that they turn into sores which may become infected.

In a nutshell: it is important to take good care of your feet. A foot bath with Quark as often as needed, even daily, can make your feet soft and supple. In worse cases, you can add Quark poultices twice a week. The skin does renew itself, and soon, the problem is history.

PART 4

Therapeutic Treatments

As mentioned earlier on, in many countries around the world the cornucopia of holistic remedies with Quark have been passed along for hundreds of years. Although with conventional medicine we can treat and cure many illnesses, with Quark we have an easy, safe and inexpensive home remedy for simple health issues. Fortunately, there are mild and effective methods that can alleviate much of the discomfort surrounding a common cold, an insect sting or a bruise. Quark has been tried and tested over and over again and has prevailed as remedies for these issues.

These treatments will help you save money, and are easy to apply and use. The poultices and compresses are prepared as mentioned in previous sections and are applied directly to the areas causing the discomfort.

Quark as a Home Remedy

Insect bites/stings – apply a thick layer of Quark directly onto the bite/sting while taking care not to apply directly to open wounds and/or broken skin.

Sore throat/hoarseness – apply a compress or poultice around the neck

Bronchitis/Cough – apply a compress or poultice directly on the chest

Fever – apply a compress or poultice to both calves. The Quark draws the fever out and cools the body.

Sinusitis – apply a compress to the face near your sinuses.

Ear ache – apply a poultice directly to the ear being careful not to get Quark or foreign objects in the ear canal itself.

Using Quark will alleviate and soothe the discomfort of these ailments and will also help your body to recover. None the less, common sense needs to prevail. Common colds, sinusitis, fever and ear aches may also need to be attended by a physician.

QUARK AND SUNBURN

Many people love sunbathing. If you take care of your skin and do not extend the time beyond a sensible quota, you're on the safe side. But time and again it happens that people forget to apply sunscreen or underestimate the power of the sun. The consequence: sunburn. Depending on the severity of the burn, the skin is slightly or considerably reddened. With severe burns, swelling and the formation of blisters can occur. Intense sunburn can lead to blood circulation problems, fever and nausea. In this case, consult with a doctor immediately.

Quark compresses can help with sunburns by reducing the itching and cooling the skin. Quark and Quark-honey baths will also promote the healing of the skin and have a soothing effect. With sunburn, however, the water should only be cool or lukewarm – just warm enough for you to feel good.

QUARK AND HYPERTENSION

A Quark-lavender foot bath helps to relax and reduces stress which supports lower blood pressure. Further, Quark can help enhance your mood which can also contribute to a sense of well-being. All these factors can help control high blood pressure, also known as hypertension.

Eating Quark regularly helps to maintain your weight and can support a weight loss diet. A good starting point might be a six-week Quark cure.

QUARK AND HYPOTENSION

If your blood pressure is too low, you will feel tired, worn out and weak. It is difficult to concentrate and to keep up a sufficient performance level. People with low blood pressure often have a pale skin as well as cold hands and feet.

Quark-rosemary foot baths applied regularly twice a week can help to stabilize the blood pressure.

QUARK AND HEADACHES

Everybody has a headache now and then. That's no big problem. But if you suffer from headaches regularly, you should consult a doctor.

A Quark compress, applied to the forehead or to the back of your neck, can feel very soothing. A Quark-rosemary foot bath may also be helpful to soothe a headache.

Quark and Breastfeeding

Mastitis can occasionally occur when you are breastfeeding. If the breast is reddened and feels hot, these might be the first signs of mastitis. There can also be a feeling of tension. Often, it is accompanied by high fevers and pain in the breasts. The lymph nodes on the affected side can be considerably enlarged. Mastitis should not be neglected –see your doctor right away.

Quark has worked wonders in cooling and pain reduction for generations of breastfeeding mothers in many European countries and is often described as being much more pleasant than the use of an ice or cooling pack. Nevertheless you should not treat mastitis just with Quark alone. It can, however be used in addition to the medical treatments. You can apply Quark poultices several times a day to the affected area to reduce swelling and inflammation.

Bones, Limbs and Muscles

ARTHRITIS

Arthritis is a painful inflammation of the limbs. Possible symptoms include reddening of the joint or joints in question, overheating, swelling, pain and restriction of mobility in the joints. Quark poultices can reduce the pain and help to fight the inflammation. In addition, metabolism is stimulated, which supports the development of cartilage within the limbs.

QUARK AND BRUISES/HEMATOMA

Pretty much everybody knows what a bruise is, how it impacts your day being careful not to bump the sensitive location or even lowering your mood and ability to enjoy your day. One wrong move, one second of not paying attention, and you bump into something. The result is a black and blue mark – a hematoma, as the medics call it. Put a Quark poultice on the painful spot, two or three times should do.

QUARK AND SORE MUSCLES

After your muscles have been overworked, they may react with pain. Your movements are constricted and, depending on the level of soreness, you might feel fatigued and weak.

With Quark poultices, gentle Quark massages and relaxing Quark baths you can speed up the healing process and get back in shape.

QUARK AND TENDONITIS

This is a problem which often appears after certain tendons are overworked. It most commonly affects the elbows and wrists, causing pain with movement or pressure. Sometimes you can actually hear a crunching sound when the limb in question is moved.

Further possible symptoms are:
- Reddening
- Swelling
- Overheating around the inflamed tendon
- The first measure should be to relieve the strain on the tendon.

Quark poultices support the tendon by eliminating some of the inflammation and by reducing pain.

SPRAINS

Small accidents happen: you take a wrong step or a little fall, trying to catch yourself with your hand, and the deed is done – you sprained your foot or your hand. The injured limb reacts with pain and swelling.Of course you must always make sure that it's not a major damage. But with a simple sprain, there are things you can do at home.

Quark poultices speed up the healing process and reduce the pain. Also, a foot or hand bath with a Quark-lavender mix works to relieve pain.

Heartburn

Many people experience heartburn now and then. It may be caused by too much stress, overeating, or digestive reactions to certain foods. Recurring heartburn is a way of the body telling you to take better care of yourself.

Seek professional medical help for chronic heartburn (pyrosis). It should definitely be treated because it is not just annoying, but also can also be dangerous in the long run, and can contribute to other medical conditions.

A Quark cure can stimulate the metabolism and set a healing incentive. Basically you should keep up a healthy diet, with fresh produce, and make sure that Quark is a regular staple in your diet.

Digestive Problems

Constipation, diarrhea, stomach pains and flatulence – digestive problems can appear in many forms. A balanced lifestyle, probiotic staples, little stress and plenty of exercise are important factors for a good digestion. The main factor, however, is what you eat. Your body will be grateful if you take good care of its needs. By the way, a healthy digestion is not only more enjoyable, it is also the foundation for unblemished skin and a fresh complexion. Beauty starts from the inside!

A Quark cure is able to harmonize the digestion. Regularly eating Quark and whey will make sure that it remains stable.

Psyche and Sadness

To feel sad from time to time is something that everybody experiences. But when the gloomy soul is a constant issue, when the daily mood is just wretched, it's not healthy. Something has to be done.

To be happy you need various things including a well-functioning hormonal system. Perhaps hormones are even more important than we thought, because when we feel well from the inside, it is easier to react calmly to impulses coming from outside, even if they are confusing or provoking. Serotonin is an important hormone for happiness. In order to create it, our body needs tryptophan, which is an essential amino acid.

Essential means we need this nutrient to live, and the body cannot produce it by itself. That means it has to be ingested through our food. How lucky we are that there are healthy foodstuffs rich in tryptophan, including Quark! That's why Quark is counted among the "mood foods", foods good for the soul and truly uplifting.

QUARK AND THE SOUL

Quark is a first-class tryptophan supplier. Its mood-lifting qualities are truly convincing. Because it also reduces hunger, it creates a feeling of contentment. A Quark cure where you include regular servings of Quark in your diet are a great way to increase feelings of happiness in your life.

TIP FROM THE QUEEN
Enhance your home-made Quark and whey drinks with seasonal fruit or fresh herbs, garlic, mustard, and spices – depending on whether you prefer them sweet or spicy.

PART 5

Weight Loss with Quark

Who wants to have a beautiful, slim body? Most of us do. We encourage healthy and sustainable eating habits in which food is a friend and eating is joyful. We believe that a person's beauty does not depend on the numbers seen on a scale. Also, anyone who wants to shed weight is better off not believing what the commercials say. The smarter way is to trust in the power of nature and one's own inner voice on the road to real well-being.

Loosing weight should be fun and easy

Weight loss with Quark is exactly that: smart and natural. Many diets around the world have included those principles. Often Quark is not mentioned as a top ingredient simply because it is hardly known outside of Europe. But times are changing. Weight Watchers USA, the weight loss system that helped Oprah Winfrey and many other Americans lose weight rates eating Quark much better than cream cheese and sour cream.

Many diets around the world incorporate the power of protein, based on the fact that protein intake maintains muscle mass, which burns calories and decreases the feeling of hunger. The Atkins Diet for example, which is followed by millions of Americans and people around the world, is based on five principles: high-protein, high fiber, low sugar, an emphasis on vitamins and minerals and the elimination of trans-fats. The DASH Diet, created in part by the National Heart, Lung, and Blood Institute, was voted to be the #1 best diet overall in 2018 by the U.S. News best diets ranking. It recommends incorporating more of the same nutrients as can be found in Quark as a daily staple: calcium and magnesium. DASH emphasizes fruits, vegetables, whole grains, lean protein, and low-fat dairy.

So what are you waiting for? Quark up your weight loss ambitions and start using low-fat Quark with its high level of proteins and low fat content as a super-smart and very effective way to shed some of those pounds and generate lasting wellbeing. Quark supports the body's biochemistry while reducing hunger pangs and exhaustion. In addition, low-fat Quark is incredibly versatile, as you can tell from our recipes. From the early-morning smoothie to a nightly dessert (yes, a Quark diet will not just allow desserts but even encourage them!), there are hundreds of easy-to-prepare meals, healthy side dishes and delicious snacks and desserts, all intended to lead you to your dream weight and avoid constant cravings. Feel free to experiment with the recipes in this book! If you find something that works well for you – please pass it on! Let us know – we would love to hear from you.

Learning from the Supermodels

In some circles Quark is not such a secret and in fact is winning supporters daily. Celebrities such as singer Jennifer Lopez, supermodel Gisele Bündchen, and even ducal mother-in-law Carole Middleton in Great Britain swears by it, as well as fitness guru, David Kirsch who was able to quickly bring Project Runway superstar Heidi Klum back to shape after the birth of her children. He proclaims often that proteins are the real deal. They are the reason why weight loss with Quark works so well. Low-fat Quark contains about twice as much protein as Greek yoghurt, but hardly any fat, and no artificial sweeteners.

No wonder Quark offers the perfect conditions for a successful long-lasting weight loss. Remember, there are many more elements for a successful diet: a healthy lifestyle and overall well-being! From my point of view, most importantly, exercise, relaxation, joy of life, love, and water contribute to this.

Yes, water! Most people drink too little water in the course of the day and also too many drinks full of artificial additives, mostly sugar, color additives, and artificial flavors. From the perspective of mega-industries the sale of these products might make sense, but viewed under medical and nutritional aspects, it is nonsense and even health-damaging in the long run.

Did you know that in the U.S., of the 600,000 products offered in supermarkets, about 80% contain added sugars, and also, sweeteners, colors, starches, fillers, or gelatin? This is not healthy food at all! Therefore, doctors world-wide are issuing warnings concerning the so-called diet-related civilization diseases such as diabetes, Alzheimer's, cancer, and cardio-vascular diseases. Why have these health problems nowadays reached almost epidemic proportions?

One of the answers lies in the way we eat, which is another reason to stop and think about one's eating habits. Get a head start to better health by eating one of Europe's best kept superfood secrets: Quark!

THE POWER OF PROTEIN

Did you know that while you sleep, your body is still working to renew itself? Your skin, for instance, is renewed completely every two weeks, and your intestinal mucosa every three days!

Life is a constant renewal of body cells. This would be impossible without protein. The muscles in your body are largely made up of protein and want plenty of healthy protein available for maximum well-being and bodily fitness.

The most common mistake in a diet is to cut down the protein supply, resulting in significant loss of muscle mass. But that is absolutely the wrong thing to do! By systematically including high-grade protein, including plant-based proteins, you can make sure that your muscles are burning fat calories rather than protein, even while you are sleeping – which will let you wake up not only refreshed and rejuvenated but also fitter and slimmer.

THE 5 BIG ADVANTAGES OF PROTEIN:

- Protein as a source of calories when compared to fat reduces the risk of cardio-vascular diseases up to 30%
- Protein can lower blood fats
- Protein keeps the insulin level low and therefore reduces the risk of diabetes
- Protein strengthens the immune system and improves the cell protection
- Protein is important for the creation of happiness hormones and messenger substances like tryptophan and serotonin.

SO WHICH FOODS GIVE YOU GREAT PROTEIN?

Proteins can be found in dairy products such as Quark or Yoghurt as well as in plant- and animal-based foods. Of most importance is the quality of the protein, the amount, and whether the product also contains unhealthy lipids - as it is the case with many meats. Proteins can be liberally found in Quark, as well as in eggs, soy products, lentils, peas and other vegetables, fish, and meat.

Protein amounts in comparison (per 500 grams)

Quark 0% fat	Yoghurt 0.1% fat	Milk 1.5% fat
67.5 g	26.5 g	17.5 g

A glance at this table shows why Quark is a top choice as a food choice with respect to protein, as well as folic acid, which is also a much-needed element for the body. It clearly wins the race in comparison to yoghurt and milk. Products like cream cheese or sour cream are out of the running due to their high shares of cholesterols and lipid acids.

100g 1/2 cup	Quark	Cottage Cheese 4%	Yoghurt 4%	Cream Cheese	Sour Cream
Water	80.53g	78.96g	87.90g	58.5 g	74.5g
Energy	75kcal	103kcal	61kcal	342 kcal	193 kcal
Protein	13.5g	12.49g	3.47g	7.1 g	2.1 g
Fat, total	0.2g	4.51g	3.25g	28.6 g	19.7g
Carbohydrates	3.2g	2.68g	4.66g	3.5 g	3.5 g
Sugar	3.2g	2.68g	4.66g	3.5 g	3.5 g
Cholesterol	1mg	15mg	13mg	90 mg	52 mg
Saturated Fatty Acids	0.12g	2.85g	2.10g	18 g	11.5 g
Monounsaturated Fatty Acids	0.06g	1.29g	0.89g	8.1 g	5.1 g
Polyunsaturated Fatty Acids	0.01g	0.14g	0.09g	1g	0.8 g
Calcium	120mg	60mg	121mg	71 mg	110mg
Magnesium	11mg	5mg	12mg	6 mg	10 mg
Sodium	40mg	405mg	46mg	673 mg	80 mg
Vitamin B-6	0.06mg	0.7mg	0.03mg	0 mg	0.1 mg
Vitamin B-12	1mcg	0.62mcg	0.37mcg	0,4 mcg	0.3 mg
Vitamin E	0.01mg	0.04mg	0.06mg	0.8 mg	0.4 mg
Folic acid	30mcg	12mcg	7mcg	12 mg	7 mcg

HOW DOES A LOW-CALORIE QUARK DIET WORK?

With a low-calorie Quark diet, you incorporate low-fat Quark into several meals a day. You will not eat just Quark, but complement it with other foods. This helps you to stick to it without having to give up good taste. Low-fat Quark itself supplies enough protein and calcium to make sure muscles and bones are sufficiently nourished. Vitamin and mineral intake are boosted by incorporating a combination of fruit, fish, and vegetables.

The Top 15 Happy Quark Diet Recipes

(Find more Royal recipes at www.queenofquark.com)

~~~~~~

MORNING:

Breakfast Quark Bowl with Strawberries and Oats
Cinnamon Apple Quark with Walnuts
Quark-Banana Pancakes
Acai Quark Superfood Smoothie
Carrot-Mango Smoothie with Chia seeds

NOON:

Austrian Quark Quiche
Carrot Coconut Soup
Butternut Squash Soup with Heart-Healthy Nuts
Baked Potatoes with Herb Quark
Protein Veggie Salad with Quark Vinaigrette

EVENING:

Quark Gnocchi in Tomato-Zucchini Sauce

SNACK:

Home-Made Cole Slaw
Mediterranean Olive Quark with Herbs and Veggie Sticks
Nut-Mix

~~~~~~

Do you want to get these and many more delicious recipes? Become a member of the Royal Recipe Club of the Queen of Quark and receive free and easy to make recipes right into your inbox.

The Many Pros of a Quark Diet

The Quark Diet results in sustainable success, and therefore, the much-hated yoyo effect is eliminated.

Many diets will offer only short-term success, requiring a never-ending fight against your appetite. Quark is long-satiating and is proven to increase the level of happiness hormones in the body. This increases the likelihood of success as you change your diet.

High in protein – low in calories – low in fats. 170 grams of low-fat Quark contain only 90 calories, 17 grams protein and 0,0 grams fat (nutritional values for Elli Quark plain lowfat). Hardly any other foodstuff will support burning calories in your sleep to this extent.

Easy to do. A dietary snack can be prepared quickly. Mix in a little water and you can stir low-fat Quark to a creamy substance. Mix it with fruit or you can quickly put Quark and protein, or superfood powder, into your blender and prepare a low-carb shake.

Long shelf-life. Stored in the refrigerator, low-fat Quark keeps about three weeks. In comparison: a protein source like cooked turkey breast will not even last a week in the refrigerator. When raw, it must be used within 2 days. Purchasing and using low-fat Quark can help you cut down on your shopping trips, because once purchased, you can keep Quark refrigerated for several weeks.

5 Royal Tips for Weight Loss with Quark

Tip Number 1: Quark can easily be mixed with mineral water without adding a single calorie. Get the consistency you love. For many people, the creamy texture is more agreeable than plain Quark. Once you've achieved the consistency you want, you can add whatever you love to eat.

Tip Number 2: The versatility of Quark allows sweet as well as spicy varieties of flavor. There is no limit to your imagination: from low-calorie flavorings such as strawberry, chocolate, or vanilla, to fresh fruit, herbs, and vegetables, everything is possible. Experiment – try and see what suits your taste buds the best!

Tip Number 3: Stock up on Quark. Cooled in your refrigerator, Quark can be kept up to 3 weeks. Since it is not always available in every supermarket, stock up smartly.

Tip Number 4: Sweeten your Quark with something healthy. During the diet (and maybe even beyond), it is a good idea to leave out industrial sugar. That doesn't mean you totally have to do without sweetness. The fructose of fruits like mango and banana, as well as honey and stevia, are good alternatives. If you don't like the taste of stevia, you might like to try erythritol. It looks and tastes like crystal sugar, but is passes through the body undigested. It does not enter the bloodstream and therefore cannot activate the fat-storing hormone insulin.

Tip Number 5: Give your body what it needs, when it needs it. For breakfast and for lunch, your Quark meals may contain more carbs – you need this energy for your daily routine. A low-calorie Quark breakfast with fruit, jam, or apple sauce is a good-tasting energy supplier. Additions like oatmeal, muesli or nuts will give you that extra boost in combination with good taste. Together with honey or jam, low-calorie Quark is a great sandwich spread. (Take that, peanut butter!). But for dinner, your low-fat Quark should have fewer carbs to keep your insulin level as low as possible. As such, you should use calorie-free sweeteners.

Your free eBook is waiting!

THE 21 BEST SMOOTHIES FOR WEIGHT LOSS

*Simply send an email to queen@queenofquark.com
and receive your free eBook today!*

Conversions

WEIGHT CONVERSIONS

US Weight Measure	Metric Equivalent
½ ounce	15 grams
1 ounce	30 grams
2 ounces	60 grams
3 ounces	85 grams
4 ounces (¼ pound)	115 grams
8 ounces (½ pound)	225 grams
12 ounces (¾ pound)	340 grams
16 ounces (1 pound)	455 grams

OVEN TEMPERATURES CONVERSIONS

Degrees Fahrenheit (° F)	Degrees Celsius (° C)
200° F	95° C
250° F	120° C
300° F	150° C
350° F	180° C
375° F	190° C
400° F	200° C
425° F	220° C
450° F	230° C

VOLUME EQUIVALENTS (QUARK)

US Volume Measure	Metric (Approximate)
¼ cup	57 grams
¾ cup	171 grams
1 cup	228 grams
1½ cup	342 grams
2 cups	456 grams
2½ cup	570 grams
3 cups	684 grams
4 cups	912 grams

VOLUME EQUIVALENTS (LIQUID)

US Volume Measure	Metric (Approximate)	Metric Equivalent
1 tablespoon (3 teaspoons)	15 milliliters	½ fluid milliliter
2 tablespoons (6 teaspoons)	30 milliliters	1 fluid milliliter
¼ cup (6 tablespoon)	60 milliliters	2 fluids milliliters
½ cup	120 milliliters	4 fluids milliliters
¾ cup	180 milliliters	6 fluids milliliters
1 cup	240 milliliters	8 fluids milliliters
2 cups	475 milliliters	16 fluids milliliters
4 cups	1 liter	32 fluids milliliters

Additional Resources

QUARK PRODUCERS

USA
- Ellie Quark
- Hawthorne Valley Farm Quark
- Oakdale Cheese Quark
- Tnuva Quark Creamy Soft Cheese
- Vermont Creamery Quark
- Wünder Creamery Quark

Canada
- Bella Stella Quark
- Foxhill Cheese Quark
- Liberté Quark
- The Farm House Quark

Mexico
- Danone Quark Queso Fresco

United Kingdom
- Arla Quark Cooking Cheese
- Golden Acre Soft Cheese Quark
- Graham's Quark Naturally
- Morrisons Quark
- Sainsbury's Quark

Australia
- Barambah Quark
- B.-d. Farm Paris Creek's Swiss Style Quark
- Quark Soft Spreadable Cheese
- Rokeby Farms Quark

New Zealand
- The Cheese Barn Quark

Spain
- Exquisa Quark Queso Fresco
- Flor de Burgos Quark Queso fresco batido
- Hacendado Queso Fresco Batido desnatado

Russia and Malta
- Curd Cheese "Tvorog Milochka"

Republica Dominicana
- Elite Quark Requesón Creamcheese
- Quark Cheese Tvorog

If you find other Quark producers in your supermarket, please let the Queen of Quark© know! She loves hearing from you and your email enters a monthly drawing to win a prize.

Recipe Index

About the Author

The Queen of Quark©, born and raised in beautiful Germany is a lover of Quark since a very early age. Also she has been accustomed to the many ways of healthy cooking and eating for generations. She aims to help you to eat, think and live more positively by making informed and deliberate decisions about your food and lifestyle.

The Queen of Quark© is committed to share her passion for Quark with people from all over the world and help them make use of the many positive effects of this protein packed alternative to yoghurt. She invites you to embark with her on a journey of knowledge, fun, delight and great eating that will nourish your body and your soul.

Just shoot her an email at queen@queenofquark.com and benefit of the many rewards of her Royal Membership for free!

www.queenofquark.com

COVER & BOOK DESIGN BY SIMONE RUTHS
www.rosavision.de

Illustrations and Images: Queen of Quark©, Envato,
Freepik, HHBI LLC, Pixabay, Shutterstock